That Lively Man, Ben Franklin

WITHDRAWN

by JEANETTE EATON
DAUGHTER OF THE SEINE
YOUNG LAFAYETTE
LEADER BY DESTINY
BETSY'S NAPOLEON
NARCISSA WHITMAN: *Pioneer of Oregon*
LONE JOURNEY. *The Life of Roger Williams*
DAVID LIVINGSTONE, *Foe of Darkness*

That Lively Man,
Ben Franklin

by JEANETTE EATON

illustrated by HENRY C. PITZ

William Morrow and Company
New York, 1948

Sixth Printing, October, 1959

To ALICE WRIGHT EATON

Who Also Received an Electric Spark from the Heavens

That Lively Man, Ben Franklin

1

Now, Ben, my boy, we'll see how well our latest *Gazette* looks in print."

Winking at the apprentice who stood ready beside the big press, the workman lifted a lever at the side. Slowly the heavy weight rose from the inked form. Snatching up the damp paper, the man gave it a glance, nodded, and handed it to the boy.

In an absent-minded way, while his quick eye roved down the page, Ben read aloud: "The *Boston Gazette,* April twenty-second, Seventeen Hundred and Nineteen."

"The print is clear enough," said the workman.

"I suppose, Ben, you'll be going over the proof before your brother does, but I'll let him take a glance at it." Striding across the long room toward a desk in the corner, he called out, "Mr. Franklin, here is a first printing of the *Gazette*."

A tall young fellow in maroon coat and knickerbockers was at that moment rising from his seat to reach from its peg his three-cornered hat. He turned and said, "Give the sheet to Ben while I'm at dinner. It's two o'clock, you know."

As he crossed the room, the door opened. On the threshold stood a young man. "Mr. James Franklin," he sang out gaily, "printer for all and sundry, printer of the *Boston Gazette*, 'tis time to think of broiled cod and apple cake!"

"Aye, I'm coming, my friend," replied James.

"And you, Ben Franklin!" shouted the visitor. "Are you not faring forth also?"

From his corner Ben flashed a smile full of mischief and merriment. "Nay, sir, I spread a feast right here!"

James turned to say in a harsh tone, "Don't for-

12

get, young jackanapes, I'll feast on you if you make mistakes in this proof!"

As the door closed on the two men, the chief workman, slipping off his leather apron and into his jacket, stared curiously at the apprentice. Ben had seated himself at a table by the rear window. Before him was a pitcher of milk and a cup and he was unwrapping a small package.

"Ben," said the workman, "you tell me you save part of the board money your brother pays out by dining on milk and a penny bun. What I'd like to know is what you do with your savings."

With a proud grin the boy answered, "I buy books."

"Books!" exclaimed the other. "Why, hardly a day goes by but what some bookseller's apprentice loans you by stealth one of his master's new books from London. And one of your brother's customers lets you read books from his library. What more do you want?"

"I like to have books I need not give back so fast. Look at this one!" Eagerly Ben spread out on

13

the table a big brown volume. "Here is bound together a full year of that London newspaper, the *Spectator*. And a wittier paper was never printed. I should like to set type for such pieces as those London wits wrote, instead of this dull *Boston Gazette*."

"Hmm!" said the workman, going to the door. "Your brother is lucky to get the contract to print the *Gazette*. It brings him in a pretty penny."

Left alone, Ben munched his roll and reflected. He had been apprenticed to his brother for almost two years. Already he could set type better and faster than the journeyman printer. Moreover, he was learning to read proof, although he still made mistakes for which James cuffed him soundly. Certainly he liked this trade better than any of the others his father had urged upon him. As for the time he was apprenticed in his father's soap and candle shop—ugh, how he had hated it! The smell of boiling fat in which Josiah Franklin lived all day, to earn a good living for his large family, was revolting to his youngest son. What Ben had wanted was to go to sea. His father would not consent to that, but had agreed to let the boy change his trade and learn to be a printer.

"If only it didn't take so long to become a journeyman and earn wages!" thought Ben, as he drained his last sip of milk. "Nine years in all! Not till I'm twenty-one. That's seven long years from now."

He got up, crossed the room, and stared out through the small panes of thick glass in the front window. Passers-by on the roughly paved street were bending almost double to make headway against the cold April wind from Boston Harbor. Capes and neck scarves blew out like sails. Ben's eyes widened as he caught sight of Dr. Cotton Mather, famous preacher and member of the Assembly's Council which ruled Boston and the Massachusetts Colony. Even this stern man, who held himself so high, was buffeted by the disrespectful wind.

Just then a clock on the wall of the shop chimed the quarter hour. With a start Ben strode back to his table. "I mustn't be late for school!" he thought, smiling to himself.

In another moment his quill was busily scratching away. He was trying to write an article which would be as gay and witty as those he read in the *Spectator*.

The single pupil in the Benjamin Franklin school had to work hard to please his master. Although Ben had read books ever since he could remember, he had had only a few years in the free schools and but one in the Grammar School, where he had failed in arithmetic. Now he was writing, reading, and studying with might and main to make up for lost time. Often he read far into the night.

Luckily he was strong and healthy enough to stand long hours of work. Somehow he always found time for fun. With special friends he took long walks, exploring the country for miles around the small town of Boston. What he loved best was swimming.

That year in May there was a holiday. Ben spent

16

almost the whole afternoon in the water. When he reached home, it was nearly suppertime. He found his father and his favorite sister, little Jane, in the front bedroom, which also served as a kind of parlor.

"Mercy, Ben!" cried Jane, springing up with a swirl of the long skirts which even small girls wore in those days. "I feared you might be drowned!"

"Not I!" He laughed and looked quickly for the affectionate smile his father always turned upon his favorite son.

"Father," he said eagerly, "I tried a pretty experiment today. I made the wind draw me across the pond."

Encouraged by his listeners, the boy went on to describe his game. First he flew high in the air a big kite he had made and tied to a stout stick. Then he flung himself into the water on his back, holding the stick in both hands behind his head. Slowly the kite had pulled him across the pond to the other shore. "It was very agreeable indeed!" he wound up.

Laughing, Josiah said, "It is good to try new things, my son. Keep on using your head to judge what your eyes see. That is the way to learn."

Ben's father sometimes gave him useful criticism on writing. But Josiah had no idea of the boy's other efforts at self-education. He was trying to gain self-control in every way. He gave up eating meat to prove that he was not a slave to any sort of diet. He stopped arguing with his friends, as he so loved to do, and learned to listen to their opinions in silence, whether or not he agreed with them. His most difficult tests of self-control were caused by his brother's impatience and hot temper in the printing shop.

Late in the year 1720 an exciting change took place in the Franklin printing business. James lost his contract to print the *Boston Gazette*. After he had raged and worried for a bit, he decided to publish a paper of his own to be called the *Courant*. Its purpose was to discuss news and local events in a lively way. Several of his friends promised to write for the paper under assumed names.

No one was more thrilled about this venture than Ben. But when he brought his father the first issue of the *Courant*, he did so with a long face. After supper Josiah spread out the paper on the kitchen table, trimmed the candles, and began to read. Jane knelt on the wooden settle to look over his shoulder.

" 'Tis a noble-looking newspaper," she exclaimed. But when she turned to her brother, she cried out, "What ails you, Ben, that you look displeased? I thought you were happy over the *Courant!*"

"I do not hold with James in attacking those brave men who try inoculation against smallpox," he explained. "Too many people are dying of it. Why cast ridicule upon an experiment which may succeed?"

Josiah put down the paper and stared at him. "Why, my son, all Boston cries out against this folly! I can hardly believe that a learned man like Dr. Mather should undertake inoculation. James pokes rare fun at him in this first issue."

"And in doing so," replied Ben with heat, "James joins the ignorant folk who fear a new idea. I believe inoculation will prove to be a good defense against this dread disease."

Opinion in Boston, however, was strongly against vaccination. The *Courant* was sold from one end of the town to the other. James was triumphant. When Ben protested against his publishing another attack in the next issue, James whacked him soundly and called him a saucy fellow. The brothers hardly spoke to one another until the *Courant* dropped the subject and turned to lighter themes.

From then on Ben delighted in the newspaper. For a year he studied carefully the gay little pieces written by James and his friends. He compared them with the *Spectator* and often thought the *Courant* might improve in wit.

Alone in the shop one afternoon, Benjamin sat reading a fresh proof of the paper. He was nibbling a large red apple as he slowly went over the contributions. Every now and then he gave a sniff which meant, "I could have put this matter better myself!" Suddenly his eyes with their heavy lids opened wide. In the silence of the empty room he whispered, "Why don't I try?"

That night and the next the candle in Ben's tiny room under the roof burned late. He was scribbling, tearing up what he had written, and beginning again. A few days later the apprentice was setting copy for the next issue of the newspaper. It was nine o'clock on a March morning. Now and then the boy turned an intent glance toward the far corner of the shop.

At the editor's desk, James and one of the men who wrote for the *Courant* were poring over a number of closely written pages. Both men were nodding and smiling. It was plain that they were pleased with what they read. At last James strode across the room and tossed the papers to the typesetter.

"Here, Ben, set up this letter. Someone thrust it under our door last night. We want to use it in the paper at once."

Benjamin nodded and bent over the type form. Not for worlds would he have shown his delight and excitement. The letter, signed by the name Silence Dogood, was the very one he had sat up two nights to compose. It was he who had dashed down the street after supper to slip his carefully copied letter under the door of the shop. All night he had tossed and turned, wondering what James would think of it. And now his brother liked it, accepted it! The boy could hardly wait to set it up. In the issue of April 2nd, 1722, Benjamin Franklin, aged sixteen, first saw his own writing in print.

According to her maker, Silence was a respectable widow with three children. She had "a natural inclination to observe and reprove the faults of others," and intended to make good use of this talent. Describing her life in detail, the widow declared that every fortnight she was going to contribute to the readers of the *Courant* a letter which she hoped would "add somewhat to their entertainment."

Since James had accepted the first letter, thought

Ben, he must be willing for the writer to keep the promise to contribute regularly. His heart thumped with the wonder of it. Now he could use his study of the *Spectator* and his practice in composition. Now all the odd and funny things he had noted so often in his walks about the town could be set down in print.

In no time at all Silence Dogood became for him almost as real as himself. She was, like the grandsons and granddaughters of the Puritans in Boston, ready to judge the wrongdoer. But she also possessed Ben Franklin's mischievous humor. Since she admitted to being a great reader, Mrs. Dogood felt free to use words and expressions worthy of a scholar.

Ben enjoyed devoting one letter to the behavior of the students at Harvard College. Silence thought too many of them, after causing their parents much trouble and expense, returned home "as great blockheads as ever, only more proud and self-conceited."

Benjamin himself tried writing ballads. Now he

had Mrs. Dogood write a piece making fun of New England poetry, and his remarks were quoted by all the bookish young men of Boston. In another letter he joked gently about the bold young women who walked on Boston Common late in the evening. Men who drank too much and pretended they were sober gave Ben another chance for delightful humor. With every letter his wit and his writing improved. James looked eagerly for the contributions and published every one. The Dogood letters, indeed, became the talk of the town.

One Sunday, coming out of North Church where he had heard Cotton Mather preach, Ben was caught up in a group of gentlemen and ladies who had paused to exchange greetings. He listened with amazement to their conversation.

"Do you imagine," one fashionable lady said laughingly, "that Dr. Mather read Silence Dogood's letter about the people who only pretend to be religious? That was a pretty bit of humor."

"Who might Mrs. Dogood be, think you?" asked one of the men.

26

"Who indeed!" sniffed another lady, in a voice matching her prim gray woolen gown. "She writes with too bold a pen for me!"

Slowly moving on his way, Ben shook with silent glee. What would those people have said had they known that Mrs. Dogood was right there in their midst, disguised as a youth in his best Sunday suit and buckled shoes?

There were plenty of blithe spirits in Boston to enjoy the fun which Ben created. But the men in power were a sober lot. Once the Colony had been governed by leaders of the Puritan Church. But under a new charter granted in 1692, voting depended not on religion but on property. The Massachusetts legislature was elected by people who owned a certain amount of money or land. The Governor was appointed by the English King and the Council was also chosen by the English Government. The Councilors were men of education and wealth. In the early part of the eighteenth century they still carried on the narrow tradition of the old Puritans. They scorned and feared any effort on the part of the people to question their authority.

No wonder, therefore, that the Council kept watching this upstart newspaper called the *Courant*. Had it not held up to public laughter one of the most famous Councilors, Dr. Mather? One day an officer of the law came to the printing shop and commanded James Franklin, on order of the Council, to come at once to the Town House for questioning.

Ink-stained Benjamin rushed anxiously to the door to watch them go. He heard his brother ask in a haughty tone, "What might this inquiry be about?" Some words from the constable floated back. Ben guessed that a recent article in the newspaper showed contempt for the government. Before the day was over, news came to the shop that James had been clapped into jail.

Naturally the Franklin family was horrified. But Benjamin at once began to have a glorious time. For a whole week he was in sole charge of the paper. He hardly took time to eat or sleep. Of course Silence Dogood kept him company and composed a long article for the next issue.

"Without freedom of thought," wrote Silence, "there can be no such thing as wisdom; and no such thing as public liberty without freedom of speech."

When James came out of jail, he spoke highly of the article. "Mrs. Dogood could not have written anything that better fitted my case," said he. His friends were pleased to find the printer in such a lighthearted mood. He sat down and wrote an amusing account of his stay in jail. For once, he was even amiable to his apprentice.

Then came a morning when James reached the shop half an hour earlier than usual. He found Benjamin at a table scribbling away like fury. In two strides the printer was beside his brother.

"Why aren't you setting type?" he shouted. "What are you scrivening here?" Ben's guilty look of being caught red-handed made James snatch the paper from him. For a moment James read in silence. Then his jaw dropped. He swayed back on his heels.

29

"No!" he cried. "It isn't possible! What? *You!* You are Silence Dogood! You are the shrewd widow with three children!"

Benjamin looked up without speaking. His brother's face wore an expression stranger than mere anger. Jealousy was written large upon it. That a seventeen-year-old could write well enough to fool him, fool the whole town, well, it was too much to bear! James glared and slapped the paper down.

"But you have always liked these letters!" shouted Ben furiously.

A bitter argument followed. Ben was called a saucy deceiver. In turn, he called his brother a stupid tyrant. The quarrel ended in the usual way. James snatched up a ruler, took the apprentice by the collar, and gave him blow after blow.

Nevertheless, only a few months passed before James desperately needed his young brother's help. Again James wrote something offensive to the Council. This time he was forbidden to print the *Courant* or any other newspaper. To get around the grim sentence, James and his supporters decided to publish the paper under the name of Benjamin Franklin.

At first, the boy was pleased. But soon he found that it was only his name that was wanted. James scolded, commanded, and boxed the ears of the so-called publisher as if he were a stupid drudge. Day by day Ben's rebellion seethed more fiercely.

One afternoon his resentment boiled over. Flinging off his apron, he faced his brother. "James, I can no longer do with your ways. You are neither amiable nor just. I'll not stay another day to be kicked and cuffed for small reason."

"What?" James sprang from his chair in furious surprise. "You dare not break your contract! You're bound to me for four more years!"

"It matters not. I'll find work as journeyman printer at some shop. I'm skilled enough. I can bear it here no longer."

Through clenched teeth James said, "The greater fool you! You will not get one day of printing work in Boston."

It was no empty threat. James told every other master printer in the town about his faithless apprentice. No one would employ a boy who had dared break his contract. Even Josiah Franklin shook his head and told his son he had made a grave mistake. Slowly it grew clear to the rebel that there really was no chance for him in any Boston printing shop.

After many anxious days and sleepless nights, Benjamin made up his mind to run away. It seemed the only thing to do. With the help of a friend he got passage on a ship bound for New York. By selling most of his precious books, bought with such difficulty, he gathered together a little money. One evening he managed to take on board the ship his chest packed with his Sunday suit, clean shirts, stockings, and underwear. Early next morning, before anyone was awake, he tiptoed down the stairs. In the big empty kitchen he silently said good-by to his home.

Two hours later he was standing on deck as the vessel edged away from Woodman's Wharf. He could see the church spires of Boston rising above the clustered houses, the green of the Common, the sober bulk of Town House and the jail. Resentfully the youth stared at the scene.

Narrow-minded Councilmen, jealous James, skimpy living, faces that frowned on dancing and other simple joys—how glad he was to escape them all! He was not afraid to make his way by himself. Hadn't he a trade? Of course, he would miss his kind and loving parents and his sister Jane. But excitement was crowding out every other feeling. He was off to see the world!

Clutching his hat as the salt breeze swept the ship, young Franklin turned his face to the sea.

2

It was a three-day voyage down the coast. Benjamin had plenty of time to dream of how he would begin life in New York. He had heard much of its trade and prosperity and felt he could fit into this picture very snugly.

His first view of the town seemed to bear out his dream. Although, compared to Boston, it was small, the setting between two rivers on a magnificent harbor was dramatic. Beyond the old fort on the harbor's edge, lay a bowling green of bright grass framed in houses of Dutch design. The place had a foreign flavor which Ben found attractive.

34

At the lodgings recommended by the ship's captain he engaged a room, and had his chest brought there. Next morning he set off to see the town. On the crooked street called Broadway he stopped a pleasant-looking man to ask where he might find a bookseller's shop.

Staring a little and shaking his head, the man replied, "There is none such here."

Ben tried to hide the shock he felt. "Then, sir," he said, "can you advise me which printing shop is the best?"

For a moment there was silence. Then came the slow answer. "Yes, there is one printing place here. A Mr. William Bradford is a printer. I think you'll find him on up Broadway or on a street off at the right."

As he walked along, Benjamin looked about with a mixture of approval and contempt. Here and there stood a fine house. Some of the streets were paved. There was a prosperous air about the well-dressed people. Yet to see pigs wallowing in the open gutters, geese stalking out of garden gates, and a stray cow meandering down Broadway spoiled Ben's imagined vision of a fine city. No wonder it had no bookshop.

The printer, William Bradford, received him politely. At the youth's question about the possibility of employment, however, Bradford shook his gray head from side to side.

"No, young sir, I barely have work enough to keep myself busy. There is small wish here for the printed word in any form. But I have a son who keeps a printing shop in Philadelphia. He might have a place for you. Why don't you try your luck in that town? Ask for Andrew Bradford and tell him I sent you."

"Philadelphia!" echoed Ben, somewhat dazed at the idea. "The City of Brotherly Love!"

"Aye, lad, so it is. All sorts of people live in peace there. 'Tis larger than New York and there you might find employment for your talents."

Ben told Bradford something of his experience and the printer nodded approval. It was not long before Ben's spirits began to lift. It would be in-

HENRY C PITZ

teresting to see the city he had heard so much about. And besides, he loved to travel. Before he left the shop, he told William Bradford he would go to see his son in Philadelphia.

First he arranged to have his chest taken on a boat due in Philadelphia within a fortnight. Then he planned his route. Without much trouble he found a man who would ferry him across the Hudson River in his little sailboat. From the moment he stepped into the rickety craft beside the one other passenger, a drunken Dutchman, his adventures began.

A storm drove the sailboat to the shore of Staten Island, where the shivering men had to camp for the night. Next day, after landing on the coast of New Jersey, Ben set out on a fifty-mile walk in the rain to reach a town on the Delaware River. At one miserable inn he was treated with suspicion as a runaway servant. When, at last, on the third evening he boarded a sailing scow bound for Philadelphia, the wind dropped and the passengers had to row. After long hours they landed to rest and build a fire of fence rails to warm themselves. But before dawn they were off again, sliding swiftly down the river.

Presently the steersman cried, "There it is! Ho for Philadelphia!" In the distance, roofs glistened in the morning light between avenues of trees.

"We'll land at the Market Street wharf!" sang out the owner of the boat. "All ready to go ashore!"

Benjamin met this command with a silent chuckle. All he had with him—a change of stockings and shirts and one Dutch dollar—was stowed in the side pockets of his coat. While the others picked up their boxes, he stared ahead with curious eyes.

Sloops and schooners were anchored in the river. Smaller craft were tied up at the docks. Fishermen in dories were busy with lines and nets. Many people moved along the wharves and streets. All this pleased the boy from Boston. Here it was Sunday and yet so much was going on. How different from a New England Sabbath!

As he scrambled to the wharf, Benjamin wished

he were arriving in better style. His clothes were rumpled and muddy. His hair was uncombed and he felt dirty. Above all he was famished with hunger.

Before he had walked a block, he was racing across the street shouting, "Baker boy! Baker boy!"

A hatless youth in a white apron, with a basket of bread on his arm, turned to stare at the stranger. But he answered Ben's question and directed him on up the street to a bakeshop open for business.

Sniffing delightful odors as he entered the shop, Benjamin asked, "Have you any biscuits, mistress?"

The young woman at the counter leaned over to fix him with laughing eyes. "Biskit?" she mimicked. "What are biskit?"

Good-humoredly he made himself understood and walked out with three enormous, puffy rolls. Tucking one under each arm, he began at once to munch the third. As he walked along Fourth Street, he was well aware that the passers-by were amused by his absurd appearance. A pretty girl standing in a doorway giggled loudly at sight of him. He looked straight at her and she ducked and blushed. Smiling his droll smile, he walked on. Being laughed at didn't in the least spoil his interest in this famous capital of Pennsylvania.

Nothing escaped those keen eyes. They noted the houses of brick and wood with neat little gardens, wide tree-lined streets without pavement, well-dressed people walking, riding, or talking on doorsteps. Snatches of conversation puzzled Ben for a moment. Many languages seemed to be spoken here. Of course! Quickly he drew from his memory all he had ever heard about the place.

Thirty-four years before this, William Penn, a wealthy English Quaker, had started the Colony. King Charles the Second had given him an enormous grant of land on the Delaware River. Some Swedish and English colonists had already settled in the region. As soon as Penn opened his tract to all people who wanted freedom of belief and living, hundreds of English Quakers hastened over to make homes in the new country. Dutch, Irish, and Germans followed. French Protestants, called Huguenots, fled to Pennsylvania to escape persecution. Ben had heard all these facts from travelers.

Turning a corner, he caught sight of three Indians, wrapped in deerskins, stalking silently along. He remembered then that William Penn had from the first made generous treaties with the natives and had won their friendship. Penn had died five years ago and had left his lands to his sons. Benjamin wondered if they were as generous and noble as their father.

All at once the traveler felt very tired. The long night of rowing, the excitement, the last hours of exploring the town had worn him out. He slipped into a Quaker church behind a group of pleasant-looking people. The moment he sat down on one of the hard benches he fell sound asleep.

That night at the inn which a gentleman had recommended he went to bed at sunset and slept till dawn.

It was still early in the morning when he reached the printing shop of young Mr. Andrew Bradford.

As he stepped in, he saw with surprise that the printer's father, whom he had seen in New York, was there in Philadelphia. Andrew had no immediate work for Franklin. But he offered to let the youth lodge at his house until he found a job.

"Go see Samuel Keimer," said Andrew. "He is a queer old fellow who has just set up a printing shop here."

Benjamin lost no time in reaching Keimer. He found the printer trying to get some type ready for the press. To the well-trained apprentice his actions seemed very clumsy.

"Yes, I may soon have work for you, Mr. Franklin," Keimer said. "I'll likely send for you presently."

Indeed, it was not long before Ben's fortunes were fixed. Keimer not only gave him a job and paid him promptly but found him a place to live in the house of a merchant named Reed.

"I'll take you there myself," said Keimer.

Ben said eagerly, "Luckily my chest of clothes has come at last and I can make myself decent."

Scrubbed, combed, and dressed in his Sunday suit, Franklin was escorted to the merchant's house. Mr. Reed seemed to be a pleasant fellow. He and Keimer talked to Ben about the shipload of goods which had just arrived from England and about the Governor, Sir William Keith, who was handsome, elegant, and amiable.

Presently Reed said, "Before we decide about your stay under my roof, Mr. Franklin, I'd like to present you to my daughter." Stepping to the door, he called out, "Deborah, pray come here a moment."

Into the room came a plump, rosy-cheeked, lively young girl. She smiled at her father, nodded to Keimer, and turned to greet the stranger. For an instant she stared, then blushed to her dark brown hair.

"But," she stammered, "you are the one . . . I . . . I've seen you before."

Benjamin had recognized her at once. She was the young lady in the doorway who had giggled at the rumpled boy munching a big roll. He bowed

45

politely. His eyes danced with delight. The girl's surprise told him how different he looked to her now in his clean shirt and neat suit. Certainly he felt different. He was a man with a job and a future.

"I'm right glad, Mr. Franklin," said Deborah Reed in a loud, cheerful voice, "that you are staying with us here."

"Ah, Mistress Reed," replied Ben with another bow, "it is good of you to receive me and I shall be pleased to remain."

Keimer shot a look of pride at his gallant employee. Arrangements were completed and the two took their leave of the Reeds. Next day Ben was comfortably settled and Mrs. Reed made him very welcome. Before the week was up, Deborah was taking him to call upon her friends. She said the girls liked him for the mischief in his eyes, and the boys because he asked their opinions about everything.

But in spite of his new work and new friends, Ben let nothing keep him from his studies. Often after his day's work he read till midnight. He meant to make his way as a printer. He knew that neither Andrew Bradford nor Samuel Keimer had his knowledge of books, his ability to write, or his skill as a workman. Somehow in this comfortable city he felt at home.

Benjamin never wrote to tell his family where he was. His heart was still sore over the quarrels with James, which none of the others seemed to understand. Yet he often wished he had news of them. No wonder he exclaimed with delight one morning when a letter was brought to him at the shop. He tore it open and looked for the signature. His brother-in-law! In some way this man, who was a ship captain, had found out where the runaway was working.

All day Benjamin thought about the letter. It was very friendly. The purpose of it was to beg him to come home and be forgiven for running off. That night and the next he worked on his answer. Carefully he explained why he could not return.

Not long after he had sent off this reply, the youth

47

was working with Keimer one morning near the front window of the shop. Both of them happened to glance out at the same instant and stopped work to stare. Two fine gentlemen were crossing the street toward the shop. One wore an officer's uniform. The other was magnificent in purple satin, with a cocked hat over his curled wig.

"By Heaven," cried Keimer. "Governor Keith himself is coming here!"

He dashed to the door. Benjamin, standing stockstill, watched the Governor enter, brush the printer aside, and stride straight over to him.

"Have I the honor of speaking to Mr. Benjamin Franklin?" asked Sir William.

"Yes, your Excellency," murmured Ben.

The Governor presented his aide. Then, with a frown for Keimer, who hovered near, he invited Franklin to go with him to a near-by tavern for a glass of wine. Throwing off his apron and slipping into his coat, the youth wondered what the visit could mean.

In a few words the Governor explained. At the

48

coast town where a ship from Boston was docked
he had met Benjamin's brother-in-law. He had
even been allowed to read Ben's excellent letter.
This had made him feel that young Franklin was
the very man he wanted to run a good printing
shop.

"My aide will send you military orders to print.
I will give you all the Government papers to print.
And you'll make a good profit!" Sir William Keith
said, smiling.

Amazed and flattered as he was, Benjamin kept
his head. "But, sir," he asked after thanking his
host for the offer, "how shall I get the money to
pay for a press and paper and all else I would
need?"

"Your father will surely lend it to you," said
the Governor with a wave of the hand. "I understand that he has great affection for you. Soon you
could pay him back."

Benjamin was very doubtful of his father's will-
ingness to set him up in a shop. But after many
talks with the Governor, he decided to go back to

Boston and discuss the matter with old Josiah, the chandler. Armed with a letter from Sir William, he set off by ship for Boston.

All his life Ben remembered the triumph of that return to his family. As he pushed open the door of the house and called out a greeting, his mother rushed from the kitchen, Jane from the bedroom, and his father from the vats of tallow. They gathered around him with tears and cries. Then suddenly they grew silent. Here was no repentant runaway.

"How fine you look, Ben!" said Jane. "Your suit is quite new. Look, Mother, he is wearing a watch. Father, don't you hear the silver jingling in his pocket? Ben is prospering!"

Solemnly Josiah nodded. His eyes said, "If he is making a success in Philadelphia, he won't want to come home." Then he smiled at his son. After all, he did want him to succeed, even if it meant he would not stay at home. When he learned the reason for Ben's visit, he said he would have to think about the Governor's plan. Meanwhile Ben went down to James Franklin's printing shop. James was still angry with him, but the workmen were impressed by the grand appearance of the former apprentice. Old friends on whom Ben called were equally surprised. He had a good time visiting around and even paid a call on Dr. Cotton Mather.

Then came Josiah's decision. "My son, I cannot risk the money to start you in your own printing shop. You are too young for such responsibility. Get more experience first. I am writing Governor Keith that I am glad he thinks so highly of you. Certainly, Ben, since you are prospering in Philadelphia, I shall not ask you to come home."

Ben was not surprised that his father felt this way. The disappointment was almost lost in the joy of feeling all the old affection around him again. In a happy mood he started back. This time he even had a pleasant stay in New York. Through the captain of the ship, he received at his lodgings a message asking him to call upon the Governor.

"Mr. Franklin," said the Governor, "a passenger

on the ship from Boston told me that you had with you a large parcel of books. That made me wish to make your acquaintance and show you my library. Few people in this town care anything for reading."

For hours the two talked about books in the happiest way possible.

As soon as Benjamin reached Philadelphia, he handed Josiah Franklin's letter to Governor Keith. But when Sir William met Ben later at his favorite tavern, he seemed as optimistic as ever about his plan.

"There's nothing for it, young Mr. Franklin," said Keith, "but to raise the money myself to start you in the printing business. Tell me how much is needed."

A droll smile curled Ben's lip. "The sum of all will frighten you, your Excellency. Press and type cost dear."

From his pocket he drew the list he had shown his father. Sir William held it to the candle. He nodded gravely and handed it back. "This seems fair enough. Now what you should do, lad, is to go to London and choose the very best press and type. Your journey would be part of the expenses I would undertake."

"London, sir!"

Benjamin flung himself back in his seat. Around him whirled pictures of coffee shops, bookstalls, theaters, historic buildings, lovely ladies, famous wits. Imagine going to London!

The Governor was saying calmly, "Yes. Engage passage on the ship which leaves Philadelphia for England this fall. We must lose no time about it."

Keith promised his young friend to give him letters of introduction to important Englishmen. Money would be furnished him before he departed. Ben could hardly believe his ears.

When the time came to sail, the Governor sent word that the letters and an order on a London bank would be sent to the ship. Gleefully Benjamin climbed on board. Before the ship was tossing on the open sea, he had made friends with several of the passengers. They all, especially a merchant named Thomas Denham, liked Ben's amusing stories and his manner of happy confidence.

No wonder he had this air. Didn't he have a promising business in view? Besides, with letters from the Governor, he would meet in London writers, politicians, and perhaps some of the scientists whose books he had read. Ah, if he could only shake hands with that greatest genius of them all, Sir Isaac Newton, discoverer of the laws of gravitation and president of the Royal Society of Scientists!

After a few days at sea, Ben went to ask the captain for the letters and bank order which Governor Keith had sent. He was told that all mail would be sorted and given out after landing. During the long weeks at sea Ben's pleasant companionship with Thomas Denham grew into a warm friendship.

It was to him the youth turned on the terrible day of landing. When the mailbags were opened, Ben's eager question was answered in words like blows which almost felled him to the deck. "Sorry,

Mr. Franklin, but there is nothing here for you, sir. Nothing at all."

When Denham heard Ben's story, stammered out with trembling lips, he said, "Mr. Franklin, this is not the first time Governor Keith has broken promises. He has good in him, but cannot be relied upon. He dreams, mixes other people in his dreams, and merely hopes they will come true without deeds of his own. This is a downright pity, my lad, and no mistake!"

"But what am I to do?" Ben was now able to speak with some calmness. The whirlwind of anger and anxiety which had swept over him had blown away.

"Well, lad," said his friend, "you are young and strong and are skilled in your trade. London is an interesting place. Now that you have reached England, make the most of it!"

Ben's eyes kindled at these words. True, he was only nineteen and had no experience of a huge city. He was alone, friendless, and almost penniless. But after all, it was a great experience to be reaching

London this December of 1724. What fine times he was going to have!

What awaited him in England's capital, however, was only hard work in printing shops. He made a few friends, briefly met a few distinguished men, and learned a great deal. For a year and a half he worked and saved. Then, with sober joy, he took passage on a boat for Philadelphia.

His stay in England had taught him something of high importance. He knew now that America was the land of opportunity.

3

The first time Ben walked once more along the streets of Philadelphia he felt a peculiar relish. After the roar of huge London the American town seemed full of peace, comfort, and friendliness. Many people stopped to greet him warmly. What pleased him less was the sly way in which the young men asked, "How went your adventures in London, Mr. Franklin?"

Benjamin always made some droll reply. But the question pricked his conscience. Many of the things he had done abroad troubled him during the long months of sailing home. He was surer than ever that the important thing in life was to do good and be good. He wrote a beautiful prayer which he repeated every morning. To understand the laws of God and of nature, to learn how to live in a fruitful way, those were the things he prayed for.

Nobody guessed that Franklin was thinking deeply about such matters. He seemed as merry as ever, and he was very busy getting established in business. At first he worked for Thomas Denham, the friendly merchant he had met on the voyage to London. When Denham died, old Keimer hired him at the printing shop to train in the other workmen. Three of them, who were young farmers, became Ben's good friends.

One day Ben was sorting type with Hugh Meredith and Stephen Potts. They were all disgusted with the worn and imperfect type.

"What a pity," said Hugh, "that it takes so long to get new type from England!"

"And therefore a pity," added Stephen Potts, "that in all the Colonies of America there is nobody who molds type."

Franklin's head came up with a jerk. He stared at Stephen and his eyes began to sparkle. "Well, why don't we mold some type—at least enough to tide us over?" he cried. "In London I often watched that done. I'm sure I could succeed."

"Well," said Hugh admiringly, "I'll wager you can. You reason out the workings of nature and machines better than anyone I know."

For days Ben was busy with this task. He knew just what materials and tools he had to have. Gutenberg, who invented printing in 1450, had determined for all time the way to forge type. One morning Ben called Samuel Keimer to see the type he had molded. All the men in the shop gathered around to admire. But Keimer merely nodded and said it was a good thing to have some new type again.

In amazement the others watched him walk away. Meredith burst out, "Was ever a man so cool?" Potts said angrily. "No word of praise for the first man in America to mold type!"

Ben drew his friends aside and said in a low

tone, "Keimer is showing in every way that he has no more use for me. I've trained his workers. My wages are too high for him."

Not long after that the break came. Keimer insulted his master workman and Ben threw up his job on the spot.

That evening Hugh Meredith hurried to his friend's lodging. "What are you going to do now, Ben?" he asked anxiously.

Franklin replied that he really wanted to set up a printing business of his own. But he hadn't thought out any way to get the money to do it.

"I believe," said Hugh slowly, "that my father might loan it. He likes and trusts you and would be pleased if you would take me as a partner. A lively fellow like you will succeed. Come, Ben! My father rode into town today to order things for his farm. Let's propose the matter to him at once."

Mr. Meredith was easily persuaded. He was always afraid that his son might become a drunkard, and he liked the idea of anchoring him to business. Promising to back the plan, he told Ben to go ahead and order press and type from England.

Of course Ben had to have work until the order came from London. While he was wondering what to do, Samuel Keimer sent for him and seemed eager to patch up the quarrel. A big order was dangling before Keimer's nose. The government of the New Jersey Colony needed paper money, and Keimer was sure that with Ben's help he could do the printing work. With a shrug the young man said he would think over the offer. Then he hurried to consult Hugh Meredith.

Hugh said quickly, "Ben, 'twould be my advice to accept. You can earn and save money thus while we wait for the press."

Keimer was overjoyed to have his able helper back. And no wonder. In order to print the paper money, Franklin had to set up a copperplate press, the first one in America. The committee from the New Jersey Assembly praised the young man's work. Several of these important men took a great liking to the well-read, amusing youth and often invited him to dine at their fine houses.

61

When the order was finished, Franklin might have missed these interesting evenings except for one thing. That year he formed a club of young men in Philadelphia. Its purpose was to discuss matters of importance to themselves and to the human race. Every Friday evening the twelve members met at a tavern. Dining, drinking, jokes, and laughter started the meetings in a lively way. Then came reading of poetry or debates or discussion of the wonders of nature and science. The club was called the Junto.

Franklin was always the leader. "Look, friends," he said one evening, "can you explain this familiar fact? Suppose you have a jug filled with cold water on a hot summer day. Why does dew gather on the outside of the jug?"

Nobody, not even Ben, could explain this exactly. Science was just beginning in those days and the physics of condensation had not been worked out. Such discussions, however, waked up the members to observe things more carefully and try to understand them.

Although Franklin thought books and science very important, his greatest interest was in human beings. Often he put to the club such questions as this: "Do you know of any deserving young beginner in this town whom the Junto might encourage?" Under his leadership club members did many helpful things for others. The Junto was known to be public-spirited and soon many young men wanted to join it. But the Junto did not take in more members. Instead, new clubs were formed under the leadership of Junto men.

The year 1728 marked a new chapter in Franklin's life. At last the press and type arrived. The two partners excitedly set to work. They rented a house on Market Street and moved all their possessions into it. The press was set up on the ground floor and they had their bedrooms upstairs. Because the house was so large, they rented part of it to a pleasant family and arranged to take their meals at the family table.

At last Ben and Hugh were ready for business. When their first customer came in, they had to try hard not to show the man how excited they were.

"Would you please tell us who sent you here?" asked Ben.

The answer delighted them both. A member of the Junto had guided the stranger to the new shop.

That evening the two partners had a long talk about their business future. They faced the fact that they had two powerful rivals—old Keimer and Andrew Bradford. Bradford was postmaster and printed Philadelphia's only newspaper, the *American Weekly Mercury*. In those days the postmaster thought he had the right to glance through any letter or paper which came into his hands. Therefore he was the one who first got news and, if he printed a paper, would always have the advantage over other publishers.

After admitting the fact, Franklin said to Hugh, "Yet I am certain there is room aplenty for another newspaper in this town. We ought to get one out."

His partner shook his head. "Why would people buy our paper when there is one already?"

66

Ben laughed. "Because the *American Weekly Mercury* is a dull sheet and ours would be lively and full of mischief."

Both young men became enthusiastic about the plan. But soon after that evening of talk, a member of the Junto burst into the shop to say, "Friends, I've just heard that Samuel Keimer is starting a newspaper. Someone has given your idea away to him."

Ben's response to this disappointment was to start sending contributions to the *American Mercury*. He signed his column "Busy Body." Soon all Philadelphia was chuckling over the sly jokes and praising the excellent writing. When people found out who "Busy Body" really was, they decided that so clever a fellow should do their printing. Orders flowed in to the shop on Market Street. It was not long before Keimer grew discouraged. He sold his business and went to the West Indies. With one rival eliminated, the young partners were sure they could succeed with a newspaper.

On October 2nd, 1729, at the age of twenty-three, Franklin printed the first copy of his *Pennsylvania Gazette.*

At the next meeting of the Junto the members spent most of the evening talking about the new paper. "It's written in fine style," said one. "First the eye is pleased by the clear print and the arrangement of the material and then the mind is charmed," another said.

It was not long before the *Gazette* made its mark in the town. But the paper had enemies as well as friends. This was because Franklin boldly plunged into the big questions facing his fellow citizens. A quarrel had arisen between the Assembly and the sons of William Penn. Although they visited Pennsylvania every now and then, the Penns lived most of the time in London. Their wealth came from the Pennsylvania farms they owned and from the quit-rent payments made by settlers on their lands.

Unfortunately these heirs of the great Quaker who founded the Colony inherited only his property and none of his idealism and generosity.

Their only concern about Pennsylvania was that it should make them rich. The Penns appointed a governor to look after their affairs, but expected the citizens to pay his salary and accept his decisions, even when these went against the common welfare. Moreover, the Penn brothers absolutely refused to have their lands taxed, although all other landowners paid taxes.

Only fashionable folk liked the Penns. A certain wealthy group delighted to entertain and flatter them when they came to visit their properties in Pennsylvania.

When Ben Franklin started his *Gazette*, the whole Colony was in an uproar over the question of ready money. Silver and gold coins were few. Most of these were English money, but some gold louis had drifted down from Canada, which was held by the French, and there were Spanish doubloons from Louisiana and Florida, the territories held by Spain. There was not nearly enough of any sort of coin to make trading easy. Big shipbuilders, bankers, wealthy men who put money into English

69

factories—these could manage their business through banks without having to use much "hard money," as gold and silver were called. But farmers, shopkeepers, and city workers wanted the Government to issue paper money, with which they could make small purchases. There was plenty of backing for such an issue through taxes.

Representatives of small businessmen in the Assembly had brought in the paper money bill. The debate on it was hot. The Governor, the Penns, and all the rich people were against the bill. They were afraid to let anybody and everybody have money.

Franklin used the pages of his newspaper to defend warmly the cause of the people. In a clear, firm manner he explained the need of such a bill and the soundness of paper money which was well covered. When the bill finally passed, the young printer was given much of the credit. Many hated him for championing the interests of the people, but far more blessed him, and the result was a very successful newspaper.

In 1730, soon after the first of the year, William Coleman, a member of the Junto, took Franklin to dinner at the London Coffee House. As they sipped clam broth, Coleman said, "Ben, your friends are anxious about you. How can your business keep on succeeding when your partner is drunk half the time? You do most of the work."

Franklin sighed. "It is true. Poor Hugh is not happy in his task and drinks to drown his sorrows. He really wants to go back on his father's farm."

"Then let him go!" cried Coleman. "You'd be far better off as sole owner of the shop. You could employ someone to be a real helper."

"I haven't the means to buy out his share in the business," said Ben with a wry smile.

Not long after this conversation Ben had an inspiration. He rushed into the shop one day with a printed pamphlet in his hand.

"Look, Hugh!" he cried. "Bradford has printed for the Pennsylvania Assembly the address the House made to the Governor. See how poorly he has done it. I never saw such slovenly work nor so

71

many errors. I'm going to reprint this address in proper style and place a copy in the hands of every member of the Assembly. They'll see what a careful printer can do."

Hugh looked worried. "But we'll not get any pay for the work. Paper, ink, and time cost dear."

Ben's eyes danced. "Ah, yes, but I hope to get back that small outlay. Have you forgotten that I have put in a bid to do all the printing for the Government of the Colony? Now I have a gentleman of importance who is backing me as official printer. This reprint will prove that I am a far better workman than Andrew Bradford."

His plan succeeded. The reprint was excellent advertising for the shop. Before long the contract for all the Government's printing was given to Bradford's youthful rivals.

As soon as that news got abroad, William Coleman again had a talk with Franklin. This time he offered to join another friend from the Junto in loaning Ben the money to buy out Hugh Meredith. Ben accepted with joy. Hugh returned to his farm, and an apprentice was engaged to help at the press. Franklin's affairs looked promising. One problem, however, loomed large. The family who rented most of the Market Street house suddenly moved out and left the entire expense of the big dwelling upon Ben's shoulders.

To the surprise of his friend Coleman, Franklin seemed more pleased than worried about this event. "Bad luck often turns into opportunity," he laughed.

Coleman soon found out what he meant. For the young printer promptly married the girl who had once laughed at him, Deborah Reed. She and her widowed mother and a little boy, whom Ben had adopted and called William Franklin, settled comfortably down in the roomy house. Deborah was a good housekeeper and a careful manager. Even if she was noisy and ignorant, her gaiety and affection made up for that.

At last, in this year of 1730, Benjamin Franklin was master of his printing shop, his newspaper, and his home.

4

Look, Ma!" Deborah drew her mother to the window and pointed across the street. "There he goes! People say I married the busiest, hardest-working man in town."

With clucks of admiration both women watched Ben Franklin's progress down Market Street. Over his red flannel shirt and warm breeches he wore a big leather apron. He was pushing a wheelbarrow loaded with printed handbills ordered by one of the merchants. As he plodded along, he nodded to friends or called out a greeting.

Mrs. Reed turned from the window and said to

her daughter, "Benjamin worked till nearly midnight at the press last night, didn't he? Yet he was up before I was this morning. He's a young fellow who is all for business."

"No, Ma." Deborah was dusting the bedroom with speed and thoroughness. "No, he studies books early in the morning and at night, too. That's not business. Of course, Ben's working to pay off that loan to Mr. Coleman and to get money put by. But lots of things go on in that big head of his besides making money."

Never was truer word said. One by one, the things Franklin thought about were put into deeds which helped his fellow citizens. He started Philadelphia's first lending library. With the help of all the members of the Junto Club, he got some fifty men to put money into a library fund. Then orders were sent to England. When the books arrived, they were placed in rooms loaned to the Junto in Jones's Alley. Anyone could come in and use the books, but only subscribers could take them out. Several men in turn acted as librarian. In a few years there were so many subscribers and books that the library was moved to a room in the State House.

Long before that happened Franklin had turned another of his thoughts into action. One evening at the Junto he set down his mug of ale, looked around the table, and asked, "Friends, what would you say is the greatest enemy to safety in our town?"

Several voices answered at once, "Fire!"

Everybody nodded. In those days people had only open fires for heating their houses and cooking their meals. Coal was not known as yet. To warm icy sheets on beds or start a blaze in an upstairs fireplace, hot wood coals were carried in warming pans. Sparks were apt to fall out of the pan or shoot from a fireplace and set the house on fire. All home owners were afraid of it.

Franklin said to the group, "Yes, fire is the greatest enemy to the safety of citizens, but we have to have it in order to live. Is there nothing we can do to meet danger from fire?"

78

The question started a great talk about ways to prevent and fight fires. Every Junto member had ideas. The next week Franklin wove those ideas into an editorial for the *Gazette*. He ended the piece by saying there was great need of a fire-fighting company ready to go wherever a fire broke out.

Philadelphians were interested at once. Soon a volunteer fire company of thirty men was formed. Benjamin was one of them and took charge of the first meeting.

"Gentlemen," said he, "let us think just what aids we must have in case we are called out to a fire."

Then and there it was decided that each fireman must have a leather bucket to dip into any handy well. Also, each must take with him a big basket for carrying property out of a burning house. Once a month the fire company met to tell what experiences they had had and to talk over ways of handling fires better. The members were proud of their work. They were so much admired and praised that dozens of men followed their example and

79

formed fire-fighting groups. Within a few years Philadelphia had thirty volunteer fire companies. It was the safest city in America.

Franklin delighted in work for the general good. He never stopped trying to get the city government to clean the streets and pay for a police force. In almost every number of the *Pennsylvania Gazette* he wrote about one of these public services so dear to his heart.

Yet he was too wise an editor to be serious all the time. He told funny little stories about country and city people. News items were written in a lively fashion. Even when he wrote about the people's rights or criticized the Penns, he did so in a lighthearted way. Using his wits and his pen was such fun for Ben that he wanted to do more than publish the *Gazette*. Why not an almanac? he asked himself.

In almost every Colony almanacs were printed. These were far more than calendars. They traced through the year the exact times when sun and moon would rise and set. Movement of tides, forecast of the weather, feast days and holidays were all set forth. Between such items were printed jokes, short tales, and verse. Seven almanacs were then on sale in Philadelphia, but Ben thought they were all very dull. In the fall of 1732 he started to compose a new almanac which would be really amusing.

His heart was light and full of joy these days. For a marvelous being had arrived at the Franklin home. One evening Ben went upstairs for the hundredth time to gaze at Francis Folger Franklin, aged ten days. Deborah was tucking him into his crib, but allowed her husband to stroke the tiny pink hand curled on the coverlet.

"Debby," said he, "I'm going to find out under what stars our son was born. That's very important. I've got all the facts together for the new almanac I'm printing."

"What?" cried Deborah. "You're printing another almanac when there are so many already? Pappy, you will surely lose money on it!"

Benjamin grinned. "Risk nothing, gain nothing,

my dear. My almanac is going to be different. I pretend it is written by a stargazer, a dreamer, whose wife is angry because he earns little money. That gives me a chance for joking. Richard Saunders is my man, and I'm calling the book *Poor Richard's Almanack*. Of course, Richard is not really a fool. He is wise and witty like your husband."

"La!" laughed Deborah, giving Ben an affectionate whack. "You are not one to think ill of yourself!"

Poor Richard was, indeed, wise and witty. He poked fun at the ladies and wrote verses about how idle they were. He gave good advice on every kind of problem. His common sense could be understood by anybody, and his way of putting things was very sly. The first dozen people who bought *Poor Richard's Almanack* laughed so much that buyers flocked to Franklin's shop to join the general mirth. Every single copy was sold, and Ben began dreaming of the almanac he would get out the following year.

82

"You'll be glad to know, Debby," he chuckled, "that in 1734 Richard's wife is going to have her revenge. She is already writing a poem on the worthlessness of men."

Every year the almanac grew larger with stories and proverbs. Subscribers could hardly wait for the New Year to come, and with it a new almanac. Poor Richard soon found his way from one Colony to another, and was adored from New Hampshire to the Carolinas. Soon Franklin was selling ten thousand copies.

1736 was a year of triumph and sorrow for Benjamin. He was chosen secretary of the Pennsylvania Assembly. The work gave him first chance at Government news for the *Gazette* and made him known to important men from every corner of the Colony. Just as he was enjoying this honor, however, a terrible thing happened. Smallpox broke out in the city.

For days before the epidemic started Ben had been having a fine time. A big event was going on in Philadelphia. Indian chiefs from that union of

83

tribes called the Six Nations had come into the city
to sign a new treaty with the Government. They
were feasted and entertained. In their bright robes
and feather headdresses, the visitors added much
color to the sober streets.

Then one afternoon a woman ran screaming out
of her house on First Street. Neighbors and passers-by gathered around. "My son is dead!" she
sobbed. "He caught the pox!" At that word the
crowd scattered in terror. Before night, ten more
cases of the disease were reported and next day
fifty more people became ill. Panic seized the city.
Everyone who could do so left town.

Deborah and Ben stood at the window to watch
them go. Men on horseback, with their wives
perched on pillows behind them, went galloping
away. Ben said he had seen every guest at the
White Horse Tavern pile into a coach for New
York that morning.

"Look!" said Debby. "There's another coach
packed with people ready to start. The town will
be empty of rich folk by tomorrow."

Early next day the Franklins saw the Indians riding away on their horses. All morning boatloads of people pushed off for New Jersey across the river.

In the afternoon Ben was busy sorting papers which had just come off the press. All at once a merchant whom he knew well rushed in, crying, "Mr. Franklin, why aren't you leaving the city?"

He looked up from the big table. "I have work to do, sir," he replied calmly. "People want news about those who are ill with this distemper. Also, I'm printing advice—which I hope all who are still well may take—to let a doctor vaccinate them and thus prevent them from having the disease. I have my duties for the Assembly, my friend. Nor can I leave my fire company."

Ben's courage was praised by all. Yet before the epidemic was stamped out, it reached the Franklin household. Little Francis, who had been too sick with a cold to stand vaccination, died of smallpox. Benjamin's grief was so deep that it lasted all his life. But he faithfully went on with his work.

Every year he grew busier. The Governor of Virginia, head of all the postal service in America, appointed Franklin postmaster of Philadelphia in Bradford's place. Ben at once set up a good, clear system of bookkeeping and worked to get mail delivered promptly.

Now he had the first chance at news both from abroad and from the other Colonies. As Franklin studied the newspapers sent from New York, New England, and Virginia, he realized as never before how many wide-awake, intelligent men were scattered through the Colonies. He told the Junto members that he would like to form an American society of everyone interested in the progress of science.

He himself was studying every scientific book he could find. He had time for study now, for he was employing an excellent head workman and several apprentices. Moreover, he was piling up a nice fortune. Down in South Carolina he had helped start a printing shop in which he was partner. In Rhode Island he had set up his nephew in another printing business which paid him well. Soon he was partner of a printing shop in New York. His *Gazette*, his almanacs, his salary as postmaster, and profits from the bookshop in his own house which he and Deborah managed together, all added to his funds. Long ago he had paid up his debts, but Deborah still watched the pennies.

One wintry day Ben was reading a book by an English scientist when Deborah came in with the adopted son, William. "What a wind today!" she exclaimed. "You have a big fire on the hearth, Pappy, but still it is cold in this room."

She sneezed. William sneezed too, and Ben, putting down his book, sneezed loudest of all. He went to stand in front of the fireplace. There his back began to roast, but he felt a cold draft on his ankles.

"Hang it, Debby," said he, "there must be some better way of heating a room! I've been thinking so for years. A fireplace draws too much warm air up the chimney instead of spreading it around."

His wife laughed through another sneeze. "How

could you heat a room in any other way, my poor Pappy?"

William looked at his father pityingly. He was a big boy now and, since he was going to a good school, he felt he knew a great deal. "Perhaps, Father," said he in a sarcastic tone, "you'd like to move the fireplace into the middle of the room."

Ben stared at him in silence, with eyes growing larger and larger. "That's it!" he muttered. "In the middle of the room!"

With these words he stalked straight out the door. If he heard William and Deborah calling him back, he paid no heed. In his study he sat down at the table with paper and pencil and began to draw. Every now and then he turned to the bookshelves and took down a book to study. After a while he sat with eyes half closed in deep thought.

Next day at an early hour Ben began to be very busy. He was off to see a friend who ran an iron forge. After a long talk with him, he visited a shop where tin and iron pipe was sold. The third person he saw was a mason. At home he said no word about

88

his plans. But some days later a mighty hubbub filled the house. Men came tramping in with heavy stuff in their arms. Ben said nobody was to enter the sitting room. Rugs and furniture were shoved against the wall. Hammering and pounding went on for hours.

"Pappy," screamed Deborah, "what on earth are you doing to our house?"

Ben chucked her under her plump chin. "Wait and you shall see."

Late that afternoon he invited her into the sitting room. It was all in order again. But something new and strange was standing a few feet from the wall. From the surface of the big, shining object came such heat as Deborah had never felt. Outside it was icy. Yet the room was warmer than it had ever been.

"You've done some magic here, Pappy!" she cried. "What is this thing?"

It was the best iron stove ever made. Ben had invented it and had the workmen build it and set it up. For days his friends came to marvel at it. What surprised them most was the small amount of wood needed to make such warmth. The iron sides of the stove sent heat in all directions, even along the floor. And every bit of smoke was carried off by the pipes which the mason had firmly set into the chimney wall.

"Mr. Franklin," said one of his friends, "hundreds of families will be wanting a fireplace like this. If you manufacture your model in quantity, you will make a fortune."

Ben only smiled. He was writing a pamphlet about his invention. When the Governor heard of it and read the pamphlet, he sent for the inventor and offered him a patent giving him the sole right to make money on his invention.

Franklin thanked him but shook his head. "Your Excellency, I want as many people as possible to have these fireplaces and only hope they will be made by many factories. Everybody needs heat to keep in health and good temper. I have enough money for my needs and have no wish to profit by this idea."

One of the Junto members began to forge a quantity of these fireplaces and put them on sale. Year by year more people in town and country all over America began to use them. The heater, known from then on as the Franklin stove, keeps farmhouses warm to this very day.

News of the invention startled Philadelphians less than the fact that Franklin refused to make money by it. Here was a different picture of the hard-working, thrifty printer. Many rich folk with advantages and education had looked down on this workman who used to bustle around in his leather apron. Besides, the low jokes he printed in the *Gazette* and almanac made dainty ladies shudder. But they had to admit he was remarkable. He had started the library and fire companies, was secretary to the Assembly and postmaster of Pennsylvania. Now he had made an important invention and had given it to his fellow men.

"He is certainly a man to watch," people said.

Whoever watched Benjamin closely in 1746 had plenty of excitement. His study had become a laboratory full of glass tubes, jars, and wires. Crackling and buzzing sounds filled the air.

When Mrs. Franklin first heard the racket, she rushed into the room with a face of terror. "Pappy, whatever are you doing?"

He looked up from his worktable. His hair was standing on end. Smudges of black streaked forehead and cheeks. But he was beaming with delight.

"Why, Debby, I'm trying to find out about a marvelous force called electricity. Look! I've fastened the wire sticking out of this jar to a little piece of copper. Come here and touch it."

Deborah had on her arm Baby Sarah, aged two, the joy of her parents. But, as the mother edged into the room, she noticed with surprised indignation that for once the doting father didn't so much as glance at the child. What was this matter that took all his attention? To humor him she stretched out a finger to the metal point.

"Ouch!" she screamed. "It bites! What is it?"

"Electricity," replied Ben, laughing. "The copper piece is charged with electric power."

"But where does the horrid power come from? There's nothing but water in that jar. I can't see anything going along the wire."

Benjamin's face grew solemn. "No. The strange power cannot be seen. We only know what it does. God's universe is full of marvels, Debby, and electricity is the most wonderful of all. Men have to find out about it."

Deborah said such dangerous things should be let alone. But Benjamin's scientific friends were fascinated with his experiments. They had all known in a general way that there was such a thing as electricity. Many of them had tried getting sparks by rubbing glass with silk and by rubbing resinous wood with fur or wool. But this year a scientist in Europe had found out how to store electricity in a tube or jar. As a result of this great discovery, experimenters had more than a spark to work with. They had an electric current which could travel along a wire and act in many ways.

All Europe was excited about such experiments. In France, Holland, and England booths were set

93

up in every country fair to show the electric tube. Fine ladies, soldiers, and farmer lads and lasses all wanted to get that wonderful little shock.

Franklin first saw one of these tubes in Boston. He had gone up to visit his family and express his sorrow over the recent death of his father. Many Bostonians wanted to meet the famous author of "Poor Richard" and Ben was much entertained. At one of these gatherings a gentleman just back from London made a few experiments with an electric tube. Ben was thrilled. The moment he returned home, he ordered tubes, had special tools made, set up a laboratory, and spent hours making experiments.

A rude interruption stopped his studies and his work. A storm cloud which for years had hung over Europe now threatened to burst over the American Colonies. War! Century after century the countries of Europe had been battling for power. For some years England had managed to stay at peace. But lately France and Spain had joined together to attack English shipping. In re-

94

venge, English and American sea captains captured enemy ships. Many a shipowner of Philadelphia had grown rich by seizing French vessels and their cargoes. Most of these fights went on far out at sea. But finally the French began to hit back. Not only did they capture English and American ships; they actually sailed up the Delaware River, burned farms, and towed away American sloops and schooners.

"Philadelphia is in real danger," Franklin said to the Junto members. "America is being drawn into this struggle."

Briefly he set forth the facts. The French were in Canada and meant to hold it. For years their traders, defended by soldiers, had been creeping south to build forts along the Ohio River. Already fur traders from Virginia had found them deadly rivals. England would never, said Franklin, allow her sea power nor her trade in furs with the Indians to be checked by France.

"War will come to the borders of Pennsylvania," he warned.

"I've heard from seamen that the French fleet is gathering to come up the Delaware and bombard our city," William Coleman added.

"And in northwestern Pennsylvania," cried Stephen Potts, "the Indians might join the French in attacking us."

Franklin looked from one to the other. "If we are attacked by land or water, what could we do to stop the enemy? We have no guns, no troops, not even guards or watchmen. Are we to stand helpless? Friends, we must set about preparing defenses!"

One of the other members said in a gloomy voice, "But how can we do it when the Quakers in the Assembly have the most votes? They do not believe in fighting, even for defense. They have voted down every bill for protecting our town and our farms."

"We must appeal to the people," said Franklin, "all the people."

That night he lay awake thinking out a pamphlet he meant to write at once. Not long afterwards he printed "Plain Truth," an argument in pamphlet form. First he described the horrors which would follow the capture of Philadelphia. Then he pointed out the helplessness of the citizens. Finally he begged the ministers to lay such facts before their congregations. The moment the pamphlet came off the press people talked of its message in taverns, at the Assembly, and in the markets.

Franklin's message frightened even the Governor. He took up Ben's suggestion of proclaiming a fast day in order to arouse all citizens to their danger. Finally a big public meeting was held. Franklin made a speech to the crowd and called for volunteers to form militia. Men came forward by dozens. Soon they were drilling in the public square. Shoulder to shoulder with baker boys and fishermen, Ben himself marched in the uniform of a private. News came into the *Gazette* office that in towns and villages all over the Colony groups of young men were drilling. That was good, but something more had to be done. And Franklin did it. He raised money to buy guns to defend the river front. Then he went to New York and persuaded the Governor to lend sixteen pieces. Once the guns were in place on the Delaware, companies of young men took turns patrolling the river every night.

In October, 1748, came better news. Spain and France signed a treaty with England, and all three nations agreed to let one another's ships alone. Nevertheless, Pennsylvanians and Virginians knew peace had not been made. In the woods and along the rivers, French and English traders carried on their struggle and kept the Indians in a state of unrest.

Philadelphia, guarded with guns and volunteers, felt safe again. Deborah Franklin put away her husband's uniform and said teasingly, "Now, Pappy, you won't have any other captain except me to give you orders. What are you going to do with your time?"

He laughed. Already he was deep in two great projects for the city. One was to open an academy to give poor young men a good education. The other was to help build a hospital by raising subscriptions. The academy became the great University of Pennsylvania and the hospital serves Philadelphians this very day.

When the almanac for 1751 was ready, Ben joined some cronies at a tavern to toast Poor Richard's luck. "I'm going to retire from business," he told his friends. "I need time to do some real work."

Amid the general surprise, somebody began to chant one of the proverbs of Poor Richard. "Early to bed and early to rise makes a man healthy, wealthy, and wise."

"Well, I am all those good things," laughed Benjamin, "so I can let my partner have an opportunity."

He settled his affairs, moved his family to a house in a quiet part of town on Second Street near the Delaware, and bought a farm in New Jersey. Then he was elected a member of the Assembly. That meant work, of course, and so did his job as postmaster. Yet with business cares off his shoulders, he had time to go back to the laboratory and his studies.

Several of the friends who helped him make experiments were serious workers. These he trained with care. Exact notes were taken on everything that happened. Franklin came to the conclusion that lightning and electricity were one and the same thing. He wrote two papers on the subject. In one of them he said fires from lightning could be prevented by setting up metal rods on barns and houses to lead lightning bolts down into the ground. He sent these papers to a friend in London.

To his helpers in the laboratory he said, "I believe I can prove beyond a doubt that lightning and electricity are the same." One June afternoon in 1752 he decided to try the experiment.

5

If Mrs. Franklin comes in here, son," said Benjamin with a solemn wink, "don't tell her what we mean to do. She would be anxious about us."

William nodded. In the laboratory he was helping his father get together the things they needed for the long-planned experiment. Ben showed what he had prepared. First he held up a kite made of a big white silk handkerchief.

"If the thunderstorm we see coming proves to be a good one," he said, with a throb of excitement in his voice, "we'll fly the kite high up in the clouds to bring the lightning down. See this wire sticking out above the kite frame? That will attract a bolt. If lightning really is electricity, a current will flow down the kite string when it gets wet."

William, who was usually sure of everything, looked a little scared. "What's this key for?" he asked.

Between the kite string and a long strip of silk ribbon, Franklin was fastening a door key. "You see," he explained, "electricity will not flow along the silk ribbon. That I will keep in my hand and the current cannot reach me. The key will receive the charge and hold it. It will break the circuit."

Picking up a jar half filled with water, he pointed out a wire inside the glass. One end was below the water level. The other stuck out through a hole in the lid.

"Now," said Franklin, "if our key becomes charged with electricity brought down the kite string, we'll connect it with the wire in this jar. The current will flow into it and be stored there. Then I can use it for more experiments."

William gravely reviewed the plan. "If you get a charge of electricity from a thundercloud and bring it back in the jar, you will prove that lightning and electricity are the same thing. Of course, we might be struck dead or shocked."

Ben shrugged and grinned. "You carry the jar, William. We must start." He gestured toward the window. "The storm is coming close."

Quietly they crept out of the room. In the hallway they could hear Deborah teaching a song to little Sarah. Ben chuckled because the singer was off key. Tiptoeing out of the house, the pair hurried to the near-by meadow.

The wind was blowing hard. Already drops of rain were falling from the dark clouds. Father and son took refuge in a small shed at the edge of the field. It was the work of only a few moments to start the silken kite on its long climb. Presently it looked like a small white bird high against the black heavens. In the distance lightning flashed and thunder rumbled.

With fast-beating heart Franklin held the silk

ribbon tight. Watching the kite sway and flutter, he thought, "Here am I, placing myself before one of earth's terrible powers. I *think* I know what is going to happen, but cannot be sure till it does." Then for a moment he feared nothing would happen at all.

Suddenly he saw that the threads of the kite string were standing straight out. "Look, William!" he shouted. "A current must be flowing down the string."

Reaching out with his free left hand, he put his knuckle close to the key. A cry from William, a dart of fire, and a stab of pain seemed to Ben one single sensation. A spark had leaped from the key to his finger.

"You've had your proof, Father, haven't you!" William's voice trembled a little and his face was pale.

It was raining harder now and the string of the kite was wet. "Quick, son, bring the jar!" commanded Franklin. "I'll connect key and wire now."

In a little while the clouds lifted and parted.

Carefully Ben brought down the kite. Side by side, in a burst of sunlight, man and boy walked back to the house. The moment they reached the laboratory, Franklin connected the jar with a specially wired bell. It rang loudly. They had brought plenty of electricity back from the meadow.

William smiled at his father's triumphant face. "Well, there wasn't much to the affair after all, was there?"

Franklin's eyes twinkled. He knew perfectly well that he had added something very important to the study of electricity. But he wished to announce his discovery in his own way. He told his son to say nothing to anyone about the little affair in the meadow, and quietly thanked him for his help.

How amazed William would have been to know that at that very moment his father's name was on the lips of hundreds of people in France! Since news came only by slow ship, it was autumn before Franklin learned he had become famous.

A French scientist brought this about. He had

got hold of a copy of the papers on electricity and lightning which Franklin had sent to a friend in England, who had had them printed in London. Much excited by the unknown American's idea, the Frenchman urged two of his scientific friends to work out the experiment described in the pamphlet.

First in the country and then in Paris the scientists did exactly what Franklin suggested. They set up pointed iron rods and captured a charge of electricity from thunderclouds. In Paris King Louis the Fifteenth and many of his court, together with throngs of citizens, watched the experiment made. The crowds went wild with enthusiasm. They shouted for Franklin and called him the great man of the day.

News of these exciting events soon reached London. Then the Royal Society of Scientists also had the same experiment made. Promptly the members declared that Benjamin Franklin was a scientist of first rank.

In October Franklin published the discovery he had made with his kite. Both in the *Gazette* and in the almanac he told people that they need fear lightning no longer. A lightning rod on house or barn would lead the dreaded bolts harmlessly into the ground. He gave exact directions for setting up the rods. Already such rods had been put on the State House and on the building used for the new academy, as well as on Franklin's own dwelling.

From then on people have had this protection to their property all over the world. Lightning had always been a fearful mystery. No one had ever dreamed it could be tamed. Now, for the first time, a man had proved what lightning really was and how its deadly blow could be escaped. It was a mighty service to humanity.

"Here's to you, Benjamin Franklin, scientist of the first order!"

From eleven throats came the proud shout. Eleven glasses lifted and clinked. For the Junto Club had just heard the news of Franklin's honors in France and England. The Royal Society had made him a member. It was the first time an American had won such glory. And the thrill of pride felt by friends and fellow citizens ran swiftly through all the Colonies. Yale and Harvard Universities each gave Franklin an honorary degree. The College of William and Mary in Williamsburg, Virginia, did the same. The professors decided that he had done more for knowledge than if he had taken all the courses they offered.

Benjamin was calm about this hubbub. To his close friends he said, "It is good that what I have done excites interest in science. But I make no claim to be a scientist. My experiments must seem hasty to those who spend their lives in study. All I do is to observe and note what I observe and try to find its meaning."

A few days after he made this humble statement, he observed something in the insect world which many another would have passed by.

As he was going through the downstairs hall of his house he heard his wife give a cry of woe. "There are ants on the closet shelf!"

Little Sarah's voice echoed the despair. "Yes, they've got into the molasses jar."

Ben put his head into the closet. "Ants are clever enough to know what is good," he laughed. "But how did they find out where to come for it?"

With a little sniff Deborah handed him the jar covered with the black insects. "Well, they'll never tell you!" she said.

As she flounced off, Ben stood thoughtfully holding the jar. Then he knocked off all the ants but one. Finding his small daughter watching him curiously, he said, "I'm going to try something." With that he took a string from his pocket and tied the jar to a nail in the closet roof. Pointing out the one ant still on the rim, he remarked, "Let's see what happens."

For some time the ant went on feeding. Finally, after several false starts, it made its way up the string, across the ceiling, and down the wall. Sarah skipped away at this point, but in half an hour her father, who had remained motionless in the hall, shouted for her. A swarm of ants was climbing up the wall and down the string to the molasses pot.

"Isn't that wonderful?" asked Benjamin. "Somehow that one ant we left told the others where to find the sweets. They must have a way of giving messages to one another."

Little Sarah thought this was only a funny game. But when Franklin's observations were reported, he was told that they were important to the study of insects.

Franklin's time for peaceful study could not last. He was too much needed for public service. As a member of the Assembly he worked on many committees, framed bills, and argued with the Governor. This official, of course, was working only to serve the interests of the Penn family. His task was to hold the Colony in check. The main quarrel between the colonists and the Penns was over taxes. Assembly members believed all landowners should be taxed alike, and that the vast estates inherited from William Penn by his sons should be charged the same as all other lands. But the Governor always refused to sign such bills.

Franklin's committee appeared before the Governor time and again. "Look, your Excellency, at our just case," said the spokesman. "The people of Pennsylvania have made good farms and have built up trade and shops by hard work. Our towns have grown. Rents and sales of lands owned by the Penns have made them very rich. They have done nothing themselves. It is only fair that they pay taxes like the rest of us to support the Government. Why should we alone pay the salary of a Governor whom we do not choose?"

Unfortunately the Penns had the power to refuse this plea. And they always did.

The argument was made more bitter by the Colony's need of money for defense. Rivalry between French and English traders in America had made the Indians uneasy and restless. They saw how the white men were spreading over their lands. They felt pinched between French and English colonists. But the French had built a string of strong forts in the wilderness and put soldiers in them. All that the Pennsylvania Government could do was to send expensive presents to Indian chiefs to keep them quiet.

In 1753, the chiefs of the Six Nations, who were friendly to the English, asked the Pennsylvania Governor for a conference. He replied by sending three commissioners to meet them at a town called Carlisle. One of the commissioners was Franklin.

Carlisle lay across the Susquehanna River in the southwest. It was wild frontier country. Followed by wagons carrying supplies and gifts, the commissioners set off on horseback. This was Ben's first view of the frontier and everything interested him deeply. In three days he was back in Philadelphia, making his report to Government officials.

"The chiefs of the Six Nations," said he, "have great dignity. They are honorable about treaties. But they have many grievances. They feel we have not dealt with them honestly either in matters of trade or land. They find the French far firmer and more fair."

When Franklin left the group of officials, he found his son William pacing up and down in the hall of the State House. William had taken his father's place as clerk of the Assembly. He was now a young man of twenty, a handsome fellow and clever. Mrs. Franklin thought he put on great airs, but his father was proud of him.

With much excitement he seized Franklin's arm. "Father, I wish to be the first to tell you the good news. The English Government has appointed you deputy postmaster of all the Colonies, along with Mr. Hunter down at Williamsburg."

Ben's face lit up. It was just the post he wanted. He felt that it would give him a chance to help pull the Colonies together. One reason Americans did not know one another was because mails were so slow and poor. Nobody had suffered more from bad service than Franklin, who had been writing everyone interested in science, trying to form an American scientific society.

"Ah!" he said with quiet satisfaction. "I know Mr. Hunter well. We can work together, I am certain."

As soon as Franklin was sworn into office, he appointed his son postmaster of Philadelphia. Deborah greeted this news with a shake of the head.

"La, Pappy!" said she. "Our fine gentleman will be strutting like a turkey cock."

First of all, the new deputy postmaster printed forms to be used in keeping accounts in every post office. Next, he planned a tour of inspection around New England. But before he could set off, he was given another important task. He was chosen to represent Pennsylvania at a conference of six Colonies to be held at Albany. There a new treaty was to be made with the Six Nations.

At a farewell dinner given him by the Junto, he told the members that the Albany meeting was tremendously important. "Now for the first time leaders of six Colonies will come together. Perhaps they will see that they had better stay together. Only so can we defend ourselves against the French and the unfriendly savages."

"Would you go so far, Mr. Franklin," asked one member, "as to propose a union of the Colonies?"

For a moment the big, beaming face grew sober. "I mean to propose just that in Albany. It is my great hope."

114

Franklin made no secret of this idea. In the May *Gazette* he printed a woodcut which was copied in many colonial newspapers. It showed a rattlesnake cut into eight pieces. Each piece had initials to represent New England, New Jersey, New York, Pennsylvania, Maryland, Virginia, North Carolina, and South Carolina. The picture bore the title, "Join or die."

At the Albany conference Franklin was the big man. It was not only his fame as scientist, inventor, and author of "Poor Richard" that made him stand out. Other representatives were deeply impressed by his plan of union and the eloquent way he presented it. They found him a statesman. Aside from that, his good humor, his racy tales told at dinner, his interest in the opinions of others made him warm friends. To his joy the conference members adopted his plan for union of the Colonies. But when the leaders took the idea back to their local Assemblies, they found no sympathy with it. People were afraid of the central government Franklin had proposed to hold the Colonies together. Every Assembly voted against the plan.

When the deputy postmaster finally reached New England on his inspection tour, he visited Governor Shirley of Massachusetts. To him Franklin said, "The idea of union was defeated because men in different Colonies do not trust each other. They don't, because they never meet. I hope to make an exchange of letters easier. But the matter of roads is even more important. Travel is difficult and even dangerous."

Well he knew this! When he rode a horse over the rough roads on his tour, he was jounced and bounced without mercy. When he rode in a coach, he often had to get out with the other men passengers and help push the wheels out of a mudhole. Good inns with clean rooms and well-cooked food were rare. Nevertheless, Ben enjoyed his travels. He never tired of finding out what people were thinking about.

Of course, in Boston he was welcomed by scholars, scientists, and old friends. All the scattered members of his family claimed him for visits.

His mother had died, but his sisters and brothers, nieces and nephews entertained him royally.

His sister Jane, always his favorite, greeted him with old-time affection. "Ben," said she, "you look very solid and prosperous. But you wear your fame as if it were an ordinary thing, like a waistcoat."

It was still a delightful novelty to Franklin to talk over scientific problems with thinkers and teachers. Yet he never lost sight of his purpose. He taught postmasters to keep strict accounts by using his printed forms. He hired more post boys and made them feel they were doing important work. At his suggestion newspapers began to print the names on unclaimed letters.

At first, Franklin had to advance his own money to make these improvements. But after four years of work he had a mail service which people trusted. Thousands used it who had never done so before. Income for the service grew by leaps and bounds. After paying himself back, he sent a share of profits to the British Government for the first time in the history of the Colonies.

Everywhere he stopped, Franklin heard people say they expected war to break out between the English and French in America. Nobody thought it could be avoided. In Europe there was no real peace—only a kind of pause. France was worried about England's growing influence on other European countries. In America the French were becoming more and more determined to control the fur trade and keep the colonists from moving west. They were building fort after fort on the Ohio River. Fur traders and Indians came back from the dark forest to Pennsylvania and Virginia with scary tales of French scouts. Backed by armed soldiers, these reporters said, they fell upon American traders and stole their packs. Murders and fights were the rule of the day.

Virginia was trying to meet this threat. The Governor sent out a body of militia led by a young planter named George Washington. His task was to build a fort on the Ohio. This he did, but it was captured by a superior body of French troops. In his *Gazette* Franklin praised the efforts of the disappointed young Colonel. He said that loss of the fort might stir up the British to send help to the Colonies.

"Suppose the French get the Indians to make raids on us!"

That is what men were exclaiming in New England, New York, Virginia, and Pennsylvania. Fear of such a hideous warfare made the Assemblies of those Colonies beg the English Government to send them armed protection.

Early in 1755 Franklin was back in Philadelphia again. One February day he hurried from his post office to the State House. The main hall was crowded. Clerks in sober garb were running up and down the stairs, carrying papers. Members of the Assembly were talking in groups. Quakers among them were distinguished by their wide hats, and gray coats buttoned to the chin. Other members wore fashionable suits of purple, blue, or black broadcloth.

Franklin saw the Speaker of the House just entering the Assembly room. He hurried to catch his arm. "Sir," he said in a low tone, "news has just come by the post that General Braddock has landed. He is in Alexandria, Virginia, with some two thousand troops."

The Speaker gasped with excitement. "So the British are going to act at last! The General will expect this Colony to help, of course."

"Certainly!" Ben added with a sarcastic grin. "And the Governor and the precious pair of Penns will show good will by refusing to give a farthing toward expenses."

He was right. Nevertheless, Franklin managed to borrow for the Assembly a large sum of money to buy supplies. The arrangement took weeks and weeks, however. Word came from Virginia that General Braddock was much provoked with Pennsylvania, and the Assembly decided to send Franklin down to pacify him. The visit was to be informal, just a call from the deputy postmaster on his way to consult Mr. Hunter in Virginia.

By this time Braddock was moving his troops and had encamped at Frederick, in Maryland.

When Franklin arrived at camp, he found one of the General's aides and sent a request to see the commander. Almost at once the aide returned to say Braddock had invited the visitor to dinner.

Bluff and portly in his scarlet uniform, the General held out a cordial hand. "It is a pleasure to meet Mr. Benjamin Franklin, the most talked-of man in the Colonies."

He waved a hand to Franklin's place on his right hand at the table set under the trees. It was heaped with platters of fried chicken and fish, vegetables, corn bread, bowls of strawberries, and bottles of wine. The General introduced all his aides. The one Ben looked at hardest was a Virginian. Tall, handsome, and grave, the young man clasped Ben's fingers in his powerful hand.

"So this," said Franklin, "is the brave officer who knows the Ohio region so well! Colonel Washington, your experience ought to be very helpful in the present campaign."

George Washington flushed and stammered shy thanks. Braddock threw him a look which meant,

121

"These colonials don't know much about the art of war." The Britisher boasted that his well-trained troops would probably crush the French out on the Ohio in a few battles. Then they would march on to Niagara and Canada.

Washington looked him firmly in the eye. "But, General, the French are brave, fierce fighters. They have learned from the Indians to steal up on the enemy and to shoot from behind trees and logs. It is not easy to battle with them."

"Nonsense," barked Braddock. "They cannot possibly withstand our forces."

Franklin and Washington exchanged a look of despair. Ben said he also knew frontier conditions and agreed with the General's aide that fighting in the wilderness was utterly different from a drawn battle on an open field. At Braddock's snort of disbelief, however, Franklin changed the subject. He remarked that the Pennsylvania farmers had wagons which might haul supplies for the army.

"Wagons!" Braddock almost jumped from his

122

seat. "That's what I need most of all! How many could you get? How soon? What will they cost?"

Franklin said he would go to his lodging and figure out the answers. Next day Braddock went over the figures and gave Ben a written order and a note for a sum equal to four thousand dollars as a first payment for hire of wagons with drivers. Taking leave of the General, of Washington, and the other aides, Franklin galloped back to Pennsylvania.

His first stop was at the town of Lancaster. There he posted a big advertisement of the deal in wagons. In York he did the same thing. With driving energy he bought supplies, interviewed farmers, talked, and explained the plan. Two weeks later one hundred and fifty wagons and two hundred and fifty horses were starting on their way to the frontier on the Ohio River. For this speedy service Franklin was warmly praised both by the Assembly and in letters from the grateful Braddock.

All in vain, that effort! One July day a weary

rider dashed into Philadelphia with terrible news. The advance guard of the British had been cut to pieces. Braddock had been killed and the army was in full flight. George Washington, the hero of the day, who had been in the thick of the fight and covered the retreat, was helping gather up the remnants of the British troops.

That disaster brought terror to Philadelphia. It made many of the scattered Indian tribes believe the English were too weak to fear. Bands of them rushed down on outlying farms. Families were slain. Houses were burned. Corn and goods were carried off. Day after day refugees walked and rode into Philadelphia, begging help from the Governor. Everyone was afraid the French might send forces over the Blue Mountains.

The Assembly spent its entire time upon this terrifying problem. Money and troops were raised. It was decided to build a series of forts on the frontier and man them with soldiers. Franklin was made commander of a company to start the work. Deborah and Sally went to the square to wave him off

124

as he rode away at the head of fifty horsemen. Behind them lumbered two wagons with supplies.

As Ben gave commands about making camp, as he led his men along the trails near the Delaware, and spoke to frightened villagers with an air of quiet authority, nobody would have dreamed who he was. Could this be the man who worked for hours in the laboratory, or sat up all night to write funny things for the *Almanack*, or drafted bills for the Assembly? Franklin had turned into a soldier.

First he put two border towns in a state of defense. Volunteers were quickly trained to serve as guards and scouts. Then he rode on with his men to the wild mountain country. Snow and mud made progress of horses and wagons slow. Often the party passed horrible ruins of farms and villages and had to stop to bury the dead. But once arrived at the spot where the fort was to stand, the tired men grew cheerful again. There was work to be done!

Now woodsmen were of more account than soldiers. To make the fort and palisades, big trees had

125

to be chopped down. Ben followed the sound of ringing axes into the woods. He stood there, watch in hand, and sang out that he was going to time the next cutting.

After the big pine had crashed down, the men gathered around him eagerly. "How long did it take, sir?"

"Six minutes. Good work, men! At this rate we shall soon have our fort."

A small hut was knocked together the first day. In it, with several others, Franklin slept on the floor wrapped in blankets. He directed the work, cheered on his men, and saw that they had plenty to eat. When, at last, an officer came out to relieve his command, the fort was almost finished and a ring of stout palisades stood firm.

It was a tired man who dismounted from a tired horse in front of his house one evening. Stumbling into Deborah's welcoming arms, Ben sighed, "Oh, Debby, am I really going to have roast mutton and sleep between clean sheets tonight?"

Before he had been home an hour, however, he

HENRY C PITZ

was saying that he would not have missed the experience for anything. To know something of the hardships of frontier life was to know America. His expedition had given western Pennsylvanians a good idea of how to go about defense. But all through the year of 1756 Indian raids went on at a terrible rate. Even in Philadelphia people did not feel safe.

Need for defense kept the problem of raising money always before the Assembly. Yet the Penns and their Governor still refused to have their lands taxed. Such injustices drove the people to fury. At last the Assembly decided to appeal directly to the King against the Penn family. By general consent Benjamin Franklin was chosen to go to England as agent for the Colony. He was to present the case again directly to the Penns, and if he had no success, he was to petition the King to interfere in behalf of the Colony.

For days Ben sorted his books and clothes. Sally and Deborah packed them. William was going with his father, which made Sally envious. Deborah, grown a bit grayer and milder, kept saying she would miss her old "Pappy." He bade her a loving farewell and, through months of long delay in New York before sailing, wrote her many letters.

It was July 27th, 1757, when Franklin and William finally found themselves in a hackney coach rattling over the streets of London. As he looked out of the window, Ben smiled to himself. How different this was from his first arrival in the great city! Then he was penniless and friendless. Now he had a well-paid post of great importance and a big private income. He had been honored as inventor and scientist. His writings were known to thousands. To such a man London was bound to offer a great deal. But that was not the reason he was there.

Turning to William, he said, "Let us hope, my boy, that I can carry out our mission here. The just rights of Americans must be understood. As I see it, the futures of England and America are strongly bound together."

6

Billy, it was marvelous good fortune that found us such living quarters."

With a sigh of content, Ben Franklin lay back in his armchair and looked lovingly at the breakfast table. It was spread in a sitting room of the floor he had rented from a widow named Mrs. Stevenson. The house stood in the very center of London near the River Thames. Already the landlady and her daughter Polly had made the Franklins feel completely at home. With two servants to wait upon him and his son, two hostesses to spoil and pet him, Ben had reason for gratitude.

William shook a few crumbs from his fine silk dressing gown, crunched a last wisp of bacon, and asked, "What shall you do first about your mission, Father?"

An amused glance met the question. "First a tailor must make me fine before I call upon the high and mighty Penns."

"Ah, yes," replied the young dandy eagerly. "I myself need some cambric handkerchiefs. You must buy silver buckles for your shoes, Father, and knee buckles also. And don't forget to order wigs. In London you will need several."

At this list Franklin made a face of comic woe. He arose and went to his desk. Over his shoulder he said, "I am sending a note to Dr. John Fothergill at once. That good Scotchman will give me advice about my affairs. He has been interested in my electrical studies, you know."

"Aye, sir, I remember."

When he had finished his note, Ben stepped to the window and looked up and down Craven Street. Neat houses of brick with scrubbed white marble steps stood close together on each side. An old beggar woman, sweeping the cobblestones in hopes of a farthing, was raising a great cloud of dust. Franklin sniffed at the sight of her. He would tell his London friends they had best get the Lord Mayor to hire men to clean the streets properly.

His thoughts were interrupted by the voice of William. "Father, let us soon arrange about my law studies. I am eager to begin them."

Franklin was happy that his son was going to have the education he himself had missed. Besides, it was good to have the boy busy while he started his work for the Colony. He hoped to find Englishmen who would be sympathetic with his cause. For this reason he was glad to meet people and make new friends. Several times a week he dined at some influential Englishman's house or met a party at a coffee house for dinner.

His first official visit was to the president of the King's Council. Dressed in maroon broadcloth, with a curled wig topped by a good, plain hat, he set forth to meet the powerful nobleman.

Ben had invited Dr. Fothergill to supper at his house that evening. When he returned from the interview, he found his guest already there. "It is good to see a friend," cried Franklin warmly. "Today I have learned much to disquiet me."

Pacing up and down uneasily, he told his companion that he had been deeply shocked by the statements of the Council president. The British official declared that the Colonies were absolutely subject to the King's orders through his Council. The Assemblies in America might pass laws, he told Ben, but, if he chose to do so, the King had power to set them aside and make new laws.

"What think you of that, doctor?" asked Franklin indignantly. "I told his lordship that such an idea was new to me. According to our charters we need obey only laws passed by the people's representatives and signed by His Majesty. Never had I heard that the King could change such laws at will."

Dr. Fothergill leaned forward eagerly. "And what answer did you receive then?"

"Oh, his lordship looked down his fine nose and declared that I was utterly mistaken."

After a pause the doctor remarked thoughtfully, "It would seem that men on the Privy Council think exactly as the Penns do. It will not be easy for you to appeal to the King in the name of the people."

"True." Franklin strode to the window and back. "Those in power here think the American Colonies are naught but means to make money for England. But I tell you, sir"—his eyes flashed—"we will never be satisfied with less than the full rights of Englishmen."

A month later Benjamin had his first interview with the Penn brothers. In the handsome drawing room of their mansion, they received their guest with cold politeness. Franklin's quiet dignity showed that he was neither afraid of these haughty men nor moved by the luxury surrounding them.

The conversation did not last long. Franklin was told to put his complaints and desires in writing. He did so within a few days. The Penns sent the

135

statement to their agent in America. This man hated Ben for the scornful letters he had often written in reply to messages sent by the Penns to the Assembly.

During the long months of waiting for an answer to his statement, Benjamin was very busy. At first he was occupied with being seriously ill. This gave Dr. Fothergill, Mrs. Stevenson, and Polly plenty of excuse to fuss over him. They cured him just in time for him to go to a grand dinner given by the Royal Society of Scientists.

After that his landlady took him shopping. He bought dozens of presents to send home to Deborah, Sally, and a few special friends in Philadelphia. Meanwhile he was setting up a little laboratory in one corner of his apartment. There he proceeded to do all sorts of tricks with electricity.

"My dear young lady," he would say to Polly Stevenson, "tell your charming mother that you are both invited to a private show this evening. A magician is to perform. His name is electricity. He

will ring bells, set off sparks, and do many won-
drous things."

Something was always going on in this room.
The inventor designed a new and better Franklin
stove. Then he took up music. One day he heard a
man play a piece by rubbing the rims of thin
glasses. Ben at once set about making an instru-
ment with special glasses fixed upon it. He called
it the armonica, and for years it was very popular
in many countries.

By his second summer in England the agent
from Pennsylvania had firmly established himself
in the British Isles. He had traveled around a
little and was made much of in Scotland, where a
famous university gave him the degree of Doctor of
Laws. From then on he was always called Dr.
Franklin.

Meanwhile he never ceased trying to promote
general understanding of America's relation to
England. He wrote for newspapers and magazines
and published booklets. In various ways he set
forth the noble struggle the Colony of Pennsyl-

vania was making to govern itself soundly. The Penns were described as selfish men who had no regard for the rights of others. Ben sent copies of everything he printed to public men in both England and Pennsylvania. Several times matters came up which gave him a chance to defend the interests of his Colony before British officials.

Finally he won a real victory. A bill had been passed by the Pennsylvania Assembly, and for once signed by the Governor, which taxed the Penn estates along with other lands. This bill, fought by the Penns, was given a hearing by a government committee. Franklin gave the committeemen his word of honor that the tax would prove fair and just. Then the officials recommended the bill and the Penns were more or less forced to sign it. It was an admission that the Assembly had the right to tax them. From Philadelphia letters of rejoicing came pouring in upon the hard-working agent, praising him for this triumph.

Three years had gone by in this way. For England the period had been crammed with action. A great leader, William Pitt, had been Secretary of State. He had brought England to the top of power in Europe. In India, British troops had captured a big section of the country. As for America, Pitt had sent over such excellent generals to fight the French that they won battle after battle. At last England was able to take everything France had held in America, from Canada to the least island and farthest fort. French troops, traders, and many settlers sailed back to France, leaving the English sole rulers from the top of the continent down to Florida and Louisiana.

London went wild over this conquest. When Franklin set out for a dinner of celebration, he found bonfires lighted in the streets and crowds cheering for William Pitt and for England. As Ben entered the tavern, he was welcomed to a candle-lit table in the corner.

"Come, Dr. Franklin!" sang out one man. "What would Poor Richard say to our chasing the French out of America?"

Ben blinked a little. He had been thinking hard

141

for days about the future of America. But he shook himself out of his solemn mood and smiled in his humorous way.

"Well, good sirs, Poor Richard once said, 'A cat with gloves catches no mice.' Therefore I'll wager he is glad England took off her gloves and went after the French mouse with all her might. It is a great catch, my friends!"

He was toasted then with cheers, and so were the American Colonies. Later, when there was chance for talk, Franklin told his companions what he had been thinking.

"England now has part of India and most of America under her sway. She is mistress of the seas. An empire is spread before her. Pray God she will rule wisely. Americans will soon be more numerous than the English. We could be worthy partners. But we must be allowed our place beside English citizens and we must be treated as free men."

These ideas Franklin soon published in a pamphlet. It was read all over England, and many thoughtful men agreed with him. But those in

142

power feared the Colonies might unite against the mother country. Businessmen were afraid Americans might start their own industries and buy less from them. People with such opinions wished to keep the Colonies under Britain's thumb.

No one wanted this more than the young man who now came to the throne of England. He was George the Third. From the first he made it clear that he was not going to be led by Parliament or the will of the people. He meant to govern in the old way of kings.

Of course, the nation was much excited when George the Third was crowned. There were processions and feasts and celebrations. Franklin asked everyone who knew the King what he was really like.

One outspoken friend said, "There is danger in him, Dr. Franklin. His Majesty is ready to hand out money and titles to all who can be made to do his will in Parliament. King George will be no friend to the Americans. He means to rule."

William Franklin, however, thought kindly of

the new monarch. That was because some powerful person persuaded the King to sign William's
appointment as Governor of New Jersey. After an
interesting trip to Belgium, Germany, and Holland with his father, the young man set off to
America.

Benjamin followed his son not long afterwards.
With him he took a final honor from Oxford University and the warm wishes of all his new friends.
This plump, humorous, quiet-spoken man had become the great American, the only one well known
abroad.

Philadelphia welcomed him back with enthusiasm. What made him happiest was to cross his own
threshold again and find himself hugged, patted,
and cried over by Deborah and Sally. Next best
was the first meeting of the Junto.

For weeks Franklin hardly had a moment to himself. The Speaker and President of the Assembly
wanted to discuss the affairs of the Colony with
him. He took up again his duties as postmaster.

Then suddenly turmoil broke out. Near the

frontier a band of young ruffians murdered a number of peaceful Indians and burned their village.
This crime was actually praised by many. Franklin was the only one who called it a crime. In a
pamphlet, which he sent from one end of Pennsylvania to the other, he reproached ministers, teachers, and citizens for not crying out against the horrible deed. This made him many enemies. Before
the frontiersmen stopped terrifying the country,
Franklin marched against them at the head of
armed troops. Even that made the Governor and
his friends angry. They said the postmaster was
getting too powerful. When he was put up for election to the Assembly, his enemies defeated him in a
mean campaign.

Nevertheless, he still had plenty of admiring
friends. In 1764 another quarrel with the Penns
broke out. They were still protesting the payment
of taxes on their lands. At once the Assembly drew
up a petition to King George, asking him to take
over the Colony. Then they chose Franklin to take
the petition to England.

Benjamin brought that news home late one afternoon. Deborah was making him a cup of tea, and he asked her to bring Sarah and join him in his study. As he looked around at his books, his desk, and the instruments he had used in making experiments he sighed deeply.

"Why can't I stay here and enjoy myself in peace?" he moaned. Then he told his wife and daughter that he had to go to England.

Wails of dismay greeted the news. "Goodness, Pappy!" snapped Deborah. "The Assembly ought to send some *young* man!"

With a charming smile he replied, "Aye, and I'll be a far younger man if you two lovely ladies will consent to go with me. I beg you to make my duties light by keeping me company."

Deborah, however, would have none of this adventure for either herself or Sally. Ben bade them a mournful good-by and set off to his ship with an escort of three hundred gentlemen on horseback. This show of friendship was to make up for his defeat in the election.

146

The trip across the ocean was very swift for those days. One month after sailing Ben was rolling up Craven Street in a coach, to surprise Mrs. Stevenson and her daughter Polly. Their joyous welcome assured him of a second home with them.

Hardly had the two devoted ladies got his books and clothes unpacked, when callers began to stream in. Three of them were, like Ben himself, agents from the Colonies. They were all excited over a bill about to be brought before Parliament. It was the Stamp Act, famous in American history. The purpose of the bill was to raise money to pay the war debt.

"Think of it, Dr. Franklin," said one of the Americans, "this bill forces us to buy special stamps to be put on every paper good before the law— property sales, marriage certificates, everything."

"Yes," chimed in another agent, "whether he is rich or poor, an American will have to buy stamps for a college diploma, for a list of goods shipped by sea, even for a pack of cards. Some stamps will cost nearly twenty pounds!"

147

Franklin looked worried. "Indeed, the tax bids fair to be a troublesome business."

"Troublesome!" cried the agent from Virginia. "Why, sir, it's worse than that. This is a tax thrust upon us without consent of any of our Assemblies. Such a thing has never happened before. We must fight this hateful bill. Americans will not stand for it."

Franklin said he would do everything he could to persuade members of Parliament to vote against it. Day after day he went down to the famous old Westminster Hall where Parliament sat. He talked for hours with first one man and then another. The great Pitt gave every American hope, for he spoke against the bill. But Pitt was ill and he had lost much power because the King hated him. No real fight was made against the Stamp Act, and the King's friends pushed it through.

A group of mournful Americans gathered in Franklin's sitting room to talk over the bad news. As he poured out wine for his guests, Ben said, "Well, there's no help for it. We did all we could.

148

At least the Privy Council means to let us choose our own people to enforce the Act. I'm suggesting the man to issue the stamps in Pennsylvania."

At this one of the men said sternly, "You do not realize, Dr. Franklin, how Americans are going to feel about this tax. Till now all money asked for by the King has been granted only by the Assemblies. Is such a loss of our rights going to be taken meekly?"

Franklin, however, thought the colonists ought to be patient. He could not lose hope that America and England would become partners in the English empire.

"The Stamp Act is a mistake, of course," he said, "but Englishmen will learn that Americans can only be taxed by their own consent. We'll have representatives in Parliament one day."

His calm about the whole thing lasted for some three months after the bill passed. Then, one morning, Polly Stevenson knocked at his door. "Dr. Franklin," she called, "the American mail is in. Gazettes and letters in heaps!"

"Come in, child!" he called. Sitting at his table in a purple dressing gown, cap, and slippers, he was reading a new book by a French scientist. "Sit down, Polly, and take a look at the gazettes while I glance at my letters."

She sank into a chair and picked up a newspaper. After a moment she exclaimed, "Dr. Franklin, look at this! There have been riots in Boston over the Stamp Act. In Virginia a man named Patrick Henry offered the most violent resolutions in the House of Burgesses. Upon my soul, sir, Americans are defying this law!"

There was no answer. A glance showed the girl that her old friend's face was pale with shock and surprise. He waved a letter he had been reading. "A friend in Philadelphia reports the same spirit there. I should never have dreamed things would go so far."

To him the uproar meant disloyalty to the King. Dignified protest was one thing, but violence was a mistake. One should act in a lawful way, he thought. Riots would only make the British more stubborn in forcing laws upon the colonists. Nevertheless, he had always thought the Stamp Act a bad law. As Pennsylvania's agent, he must do as the Assembly asked and work to get Parliament to repeal the Act.

Long before American agents could do much, they learned that resistance was spreading through the Colonies. Franklin read with horror that Boston mobs had gone wild. Stirred up by the flaming speeches of a man named Samuel Adams, crowds had torn down the Governor's house and flung his fine books into the street. When the stamps arrived in New York, a band of rioters made off with the Governor's chariot, set a stuffed image of him on the seat, and then set the image afire as they dragged it through the streets. Resolutions against the Act were passed by one Assembly after another. A Stamp Act Congress with representatives from nine Colonies met in New York to demand repeal. In many cities men were joining a group called the Sons of Liberty, determined to defend their rights.

As for Pennsylvania, crowds almost mobbed the

man who was to give out the stamps. People knew that Franklin had chosen him. Many said that Franklin had wanted the Stamp Act and was paid to help get it passed. A crowd surrounded the new house into which Deborah and Sally had just moved on Market Street. "We'll burn it down!" they yelled.

Mrs. Stevenson and her daughter were horrified at this report. "What did your poor wife do?" they asked.

Ben grinned proudly. "Debby sent our daughter off to William in New Jersey. But she herself stayed at home, gun in hand, with her brothers also armed and ready to defend the house. She wouldn't let anybody touch her old Pappy's books and queer machines. Not she!"

In his heart he was greatly worried. But most of the Assembly members trusted him completely. They knew he was working might and main to get the Stamp Act repealed.

A considerable number of Parliament members listened to him with sympathy. These were tradesmen and manufacturers. They also hated the Stamp Act, for now Americans were refusing to buy any English goods. Women were making gowns and men's suits of homespun linen and wool. Families were doing without tea and damask curtains and new furniture. British ships packed with goods had to turn around and sail home. Consequently howls of despair from merchants all over England were now heard in Westminster Hall.

Little by little, leaders of Parliament began to think the Stamp Act was too drastic. They even told the King so. Finally it was agreed to invite those who opposed the Stamp Act to come before Parliament and state their case. On February 12th and 13th, 1766, Benjamin Franklin was called before the House of Commons to answer questions about American affairs.

There he stood, facing the lawmakers of the British Empire. He was not at all nervous. In the first place, he felt rather superior to the many members who had taken bribes from the King. This was anything but an honest Parliament and all America knew it. In the second place, Franklin was well prepared for the examination. He had worked out a nice little plot. With a number of the members who wanted repeal he had discussed the questions they ought to ask. So he knew what was coming and had the answers ready.

In a short time the questions and answers had brought out three important facts. One, Americans themselves had spent large sums on the French and Indian War and thought it unfair to be taxed further. Two, many frontiersmen and farmers could not afford to buy the stamps. Three, the tax was against the charter rights of the Colonies to vote on all taxes.

Then the men who had pushed the bill began questioning Franklin. The Secretary of State asked, "Would not the Americans agree to a more moderate tax?"

"No, never," replied Franklin quietly, "unless compelled by force of arms."

For hours the questioning went on. Franklin was never at a loss. He could not be trapped. Facts and figures were at his finger tips. He knew the frontier, the villages and towns, the temper of the people from New England to South Carolina. Not only had he traveled over the country; he had read the local gazettes and exchanged letters with scores of leaders. Quietly and reasonably he spoke for the rights of citizens and for justice in government.

From that day on Franklin had a new kind of fame. The series of questions and answers was reported in full and was published word for word. First it appeared in London, then in Boston, New York, Philadelphia, Williamsburg, capital of Virginia, and in New London, Connecticut. Later it was translated into French and read in Europe. Dr. Franklin was now celebrated as the defender of liberty, the statesman, the person who knew more about America than anyone else.

In March, 1766, the Stamp Act was repealed. In high spirits the Americans in London gathered about Ben Franklin. "To you, the hero of the victory!" they cried, lifting their wineglasses in a toast. That was what they said in America when news of repeal reached its shores. Bonfires, processions, feasts, every kind of celebration went on in each Colony. And Franklin's name was cheered to the echo.

Yet if any visitor called unexpectedly at the house on Craven Street, he was likely to find the famous man merely having a good time. One member of Parliament, ushered to the door of his apartment, was amazed to hear inside the sound of girlish laughter. He knocked and a voice called out, "Come in! Come in!"

There was Dr. Franklin, wrapped in a dressing gown and without his wig. On each side of him was a pretty girl, Polly Stevenson and her best friend. Still laughing, the portly figure arose to greet the visitor.

"Princess Mary of the House of Stevenson and her handmaiden, sir!" said Franklin with a wave of the hand. "What a pity the Queen, her mother, is absent!"

Dr. Fothergill, however, found his friend in

quite another state of mind one evening at dinner. He said to Ben, "You must be a proud man to have done so much for the repeal."

Benjamin shook his head. "I am a troubled man," he replied gravely. "I fear I must give up my dream of union between England and America within a great empire. The British Government refuses to see that the colonists cannot be forced to obey laws they've had no voice in making. Another tax will be tried. The colonists will again resist. And where, my friend, is this going to end?"

7

Returning from a three months' trip
to Germany in 1768, Franklin was welcomed at
dinner by his hostess, Mrs. Stevenson. He missed
Polly, who was now living with her aunt, but was
glad to have a friend to share his exciting news
from home.

"My daughter Sally is going to be married," he
said. "One Richard Bache, a merchant, who seems
to be a good fellow, is the bridegroom."

Asked if he didn't long to go back for the wed-
ding, he answered that he did indeed. However,
not only did Pennsylvania insist on his remaining

as the colonial agent, but Georgia, New Jersey, and Massachusetts all seemed likely to ask him to look after their interests.

"The Colonies are at peace since the repeal of the Stamp Act," said he, "but they think Parliament had better be watched."

Franklin's friends close to the court and to Parliamentary leaders told him about the plans for a new tax. A man named Charles Townshend was in charge of raising and spending money. He was pushing through Parliament a series of taxes for America on tea, glass, paper, and paint. The money thus raised was to pay for governors and judges who were to be sent out from England.

Townshend's tax bill troubled the Secretary of State for the Colonies. He had a long conference with Franklin about it.

"You see, my lord," said Ben, "Americans are not in fact dependent on England as once they were. They can manufacture things. They actually do produce most of their foodstuffs, except spices, tea, sugar, and coffee. Yet England insists that we import quantities of goods, and always in British ships. If a Philadelphia merchant orders wine and oil from Portugal, he cannot get it direct from that country. These products must first go to England and then be brought over in English vessels. This makes extra cost. For years our people have submitted to such orders with mere grumbling. But now, if taxes are laid on needed imports, if money taken from our pockets without our consent is to pay governors and judges chosen by England, all Americans will be enraged."

The friendly Secretary listened thoughtfully. "All Americans?" he repeated. "Or only ignorant mobs?"

"My lord," Franklin said earnestly, "a few amongst us are so blind as to feel that everything England does is right. But the men who protest acts of tyranny are rich planters like Mr. George Washington, shrewd bankers and merchants, men of education and character. They speak in their petitions of liberty. They want freedom not only in government but in making a good living. Yet

160

remember, sir, that nevertheless Americans are still loyal to the King. Good sense and just laws will hold them by natural ties to the mother country."

As time went on, Franklin saw that good sense was not to be found in Parliament. When a storm of protest over the Townshend Acts swept from America across the sea, King George and his supporters would not admit they had made foolish laws. They only grew angry and called the colonists rebels. This surprised Americans, who believed themselves loyal subjects of the King, wishing only the same rights that English subjects had.

No one worried over these discords more than Franklin. In his long letters to American leaders he kept urging patience. In the articles he wrote for the English public in London papers, he explained the rights of the Colonies. Always he worked for mutual understanding.

But anxiety never stopped him from living, laughing, and having fun. With a great friend who was the Queen's physician, he dashed over for a first visit to Paris. Scientists and people of importance welcomed him with open arms. He was presented to King Louis the Fifteenth, bought new clothes, had his portrait painted, and enjoyed every moment. He wrote Polly Stevenson that French women dabbed a round patch of red on their cheeks. He praised French manners to the skies and added that he had been changed into a Frenchman by his tailor and wig-maker.

"Only think what a figure I make in a little bag-wig and naked ears! They told me I was become twenty years younger and looked very galante."

In England, also, he had plenty of lively moments. His rich and powerful friends invited him to their country houses. Everywhere he went, he tried to spread understanding of America's problems. This was no easy task. For Englishmen were tired of the unrest in America.

Year by year violence increased there. New York refused to house British soldiers. In Providence a

British government ship, sent to spy on smugglers and collect revenues, was burned. Boston was ever in a state of riot. British troops filled the town. One clash between soldiers and a group of nagging youths ended in the death of four Americans and the wounding of seven others. Sam Adams called this a "massacre," and people looked with hatred at the soldiers in red coats.

Franklin took good care to tell the English how well the American boycott of British merchandise was going. "Tea drinking is scorned," he said. "The most elegant ladies and gentlemen go to balls in their old clothes and in homespun. British merchants must be losing a vast amount of trade."

Dr. Fothergill often came to Franklin's house to read the American gazettes. He said to Ben, "How you have changed, my friend, about uprisings in your country since the Stamp Act riots."

Franklin's eyes twinkled behind his spectacles. "I ask myself how I'd feel if British soldiers were quartered in my house. Imagine my good, tempery Debby waiting upon them! Ah, it is hard to be

163

patient with the stupid acts of Parliament. They are bound to be resisted."

In 1770 the Townshend Acts were repealed. But this time there was no rejoicing in America. In the first place, a tax was still left on tea. Thus Parliament made it clear that it meant to tax the Colonies. In the second place, troops had seized Boston's chief fort in the harbor, called the Castle, and could therefore command both town and port. All the other Colonies resented this move and watched Massachusetts with warm sympathy.

In the next two years Franklin's constant activity made him very important. If he was not presenting a petition, he was printing pieces to make fun of English methods of government, which made everybody except the angry ministers roar with laughter. The King and his advisers believed this man urged the Colonies to violence and they longed for a chance to humble him. Suddenly they found an excuse to do so. They discovered something that Franklin had done two years before which could be considered serious misconduct.

An Englishman had given Franklin a packet of letters written by the Governor of Massachusetts to an official in England. These letters plainly showed that the Governor, although American born, had suggested to the British ministers some of the very worst acts they undertook. Franklin sent the letters to a leader of the Massachusetts Assembly, asking that they be shown only to a few other leaders in great secrecy and that they never be printed. He did this because he felt it would make American leaders more patient with Parliament. If Englishmen followed suggestions of American-born officials, they were not so much to blame for their deeds. Franklin never gave up hope that if only enough men on both sides would be reasonable, a serious split could be avoided.

What happened was exactly the opposite of Ben's intention. The Governor's letters were passed around Boston from one to another, were read in the Assembly, and finally printed. A roar of rage went up, and the Assemblymen sent a petition to King George asking that the Governor and his assistant be removed. Of course it was noised about that the letters caused this angry demand for a change of Governors.

At first someone else, not Franklin, was blamed for letting the letters reach Boston. A great scandal followed and even a duel took place. Whereupon Franklin announced publicly that he alone was to blame for sending the Governor's letters. He explained his purpose in so doing, stated that he did not regard the letters as private in the ordinary sense, since they were written by one public man to another public man, and firmly refused to tell who gave them to him.

Now, at last, the British Government had an opportunity to pounce upon the man so hateful to it. In January, 1774, Franklin received a summons to appear before His Majesty's Privy Council for Plantation Affairs. The declared purpose of the summons was to discuss the petition from the Massachusetts Assembly, but at a short hearing Ben was warned that he had to answer for possession and transfer of the Governor's letters.

Ben's friends were much worried. "Oh, well," he sighed, "men in public life are always being attacked. I have done nothing to be ashamed of. I shall always protect the man who gave me the letters in the first place."

He did engage a lawyer, but he had little faith in any possible defense. He had taken the blame and refused to accuse anyone else. It was a bad moment, of course, but it did not seem likely that the British would send him to the Tower of London, that famous prison, as hotheads suggested.

In the midst of his conferences with the lawyer, startling news came from America. Ben had gone to a small gathering of friends one afternoon and was met at the very door by excited questions. "Have you seen the journals?" "Did you hear what happened in Boston?"

Then and there he learned of the Boston Tea Party. Three shiploads of tea, just arrived from England, had been dumped into Boston Harbor by a group of angry citizens. Ben listened to this in shocked surprise. "This is an outrage!"

167

he declared. "The city should pay for the tea."

To his friend Fothergill he added in a low tone, "Such a wicked deed will make the government men more bitter against me than ever."

When the day of the examination came, Franklin went alone to the room of the Privy Council. Already the hallway outside was jammed with men in high office and with titled gentlemen and friends of the King. Inside, the Council members, some thirty-six in all, sat at a long table. There were no seats for visitors, but they crowded into the room. Franklin took his stand near the fireplace, facing them all. He wore a suit of figured velvet from the English manufacturing town of Manchester. His fine, ruffled shirt, his well-curled wig, his gleaming white stockings all added to the impression of quiet dignity he was making.

When the Council president opened the meeting, the petition from Massachusetts was read. Next the letters were read. Then Ben's lawyer stated that, in presenting their petition, the Assembly of the Colony had appealed to the King's wisdom and goodness for the removal of the Governor in order to restore order.

Now it was the turn of the prosecutor for the King. For nearly an hour he raged and roared at Franklin. Thumping the table, calling him a thief and declaring him a man without honor, a man who deliberately set Massachusetts aflame and then felt quite at ease, the prosecutor heaped one insult after another upon America's most famous and distinguished citizen.

With tilted chin and calm eyes, Benjamin Franklin stood motionless. His expression did not change. The anger which seethed in his veins at these false and insolent charges was kept down so firmly that color never even rose to his cheeks. With superb dignity he let the tide of hate beat upon him. His silence shamed the noisy tirade. It showed a magnificent contempt.

At last the prosecutor folded up his papers. Men pressed about him with praise for his eloquence. Franklin picked up his hat and quietly walked away, alone as he had come.

Next morning he had breakfast at the house of a famous scientist who was his friend. The man had been at the Council meeting and was in a fine fury against the prosecutor. "It was an outrage!" he cried. "Many of the men there, even if they dared not speak or had no chance to do so, are sorely disturbed."

Calmly Franklin helped himself to a little more kidney stew. "It would have been unbearable had I not a clear conscience. As I grow older, I grow less concerned about ill-placed blame."

To other friends who came to see Ben that Sunday he said the same thing. Most of them thought the prosecutor hurt the King's cause far more than he hurt Franklin. But on Monday a fresh blow was delivered to the hated agent of four Colonies. Franklin was dismissed from his office as deputy postmaster. It was harder to shrug this off. But, after all, he had his salaries from the various Assemblies and his private income. And he was busy enough without supervising the accounts and affairs of the post offices.

170

Horrified as Ben had been over the destruction of the tea, he was even more pained by the British Government's revenge. The Massachusetts Colony charter was suspended and the harbor was closed to all ships.

"These harsh measures," he told his friends in Parliament, "will unite the Colonies as never before. I hear that the people of Virginia, Connecticut, and even South Carolina are sending Massachusetts great quantities of food and materials. Pennsylvania sends money. Protests come in by every mail."

By every mail also came warm praise of Franklin. His persecution at the hands of the King's ministers made him a hero in the eyes of Americans. This was lucky. For one of the colonial agents in London, a man named Arthur Lee, had been sending back to America letters full of jealous suspicions of Franklin's behavior. He accused him of serving British interests. But the accusations fell on deaf ears.

Franklin always rejoiced when a letter came

from Deborah. She was very happy in her daughter's marriage. Now Sarah Bache had a little son named Benjamin, whose every act was reported by his doting grandmother. It was not long before Ben wrote her similar news. His young friend Polly Stevenson, who had married a doctor and lived in Craven Street, also had a baby son. Ben was his godfather and delighted in writing Deborah how the baby sat on his knee and played with his big gold watch.

When Parliament was not meeting, Benjamin traveled. He went to Paris again and had an even better time than before. He visited the manufacturing towns of England and made a long stay in Ireland, where he found warm friendship for America. In his leisure time he made some new experiments and had his scientific notes published both in England and France. On a visit to the beautiful country home of a bishop who grew to be his close friend, he began to write the story of his life—one of the world's most famous books.

By the summer of 1774, many powerful Eng-

172

lishmen were alarmed at the widening split between England and her rich Colonies. Several of them turned to Franklin for ideas as to how to make peace. They got no soft answers.

"England must lead the way," said he, "by taking her troops out of Boston, opening the harbor to shipping, and giving the city back its fort. When that is done, I myself will urge Massachusetts to pay for the ruined tea."

He was asked if the Colony would really foot the bill. "I believe so," he answered. "Indeed, if the British Government will do as I advise and show herself generous, I'll pledge my personal fortune for the payment of the tea."

Now came word of the very union which Franklin had foretold. The First Continental Congress with delegates from all the Colonies met in Philadelphia in September of 1774. There a resolution was drawn up and sent to Franklin to be taken to King George. Franklin tested it out by showing it to the wise William Pitt, who had been given the title of Lord Chatham.

When Chatham had read it, he said, "The Continental Congress is the most honorable assembly of statesmen since those of the ancient Greeks and Romans."

But neither great nor small friends of America could make the royal ministers accept a generous plan for pacifying the Colonies. Instead, they wished only to humble and punish them. In secret, two men close to the inner circles of government came to talk to Franklin. They tried to persuade him to make Massachusetts yield.

From one interview he came away in a state of great indignation. One of the American agents happened to be waiting in his drawing room to see him. "Dr. Franklin!" exclaimed the man. "You look much disturbed. What has happened?"

Usually Ben was reserved about politics. But this time he was in too much of a temper to keep silent. "They have tried to bribe me!" he burst out. "British officials will do anything except something sensible and fair."

Week by week Franklin grew more hopeless.

174

"We are drifting toward war," he told his friends anxiously. Often when he read American gazettes the tears rolled down his cheeks. He pictured his beloved country torn by battles.

Early in 1775 Franklin saw in his packet of mail a letter in the handwriting of his daughter Sarah. She wrote seldom and, startled and anxious, he held the letter in his hands a moment to prepare himself for bad news. There it was. Simply and sadly Sally wrote that Deborah had suddenly died. For hours Ben sat thinking of the long companionship which, even in absence, always seemed so warm and close.

He was going home again at last. What a huge packing of books and papers! How many farewell visits and letters! In ten years he had almost taken root in London. It was hard to leave. He scarcely knew what awaited him in America. On the 5th of May he reached Philadelphia.

An eager crowd was waiting for him and cheering for him. Amid a babble of greetings excited voices kept telling him of recent events.

"There has been a battle in Massachusetts. At Lexington and Concord the British troops were cut in pieces."

"Virginia's Governor has turned the palace at Williamsburg into a fort. He is there with captured guns, defending himself against a possible outbreak of the people."

"Wait till you see our troops! Companies are drilling in every Colony. We'll show those redcoats what we're made of!"

On the way to his house Franklin learned that the Second Continental Congress was about to meet at the Philadelphia State House. For hours people trooped in to see him. Hardly one of them asked him about his work in London or about Parliament. They were too much stirred by what was happening in America.

Ben said little. He wanted time to think. Deep in him somewhere sounded the question, Is there no hope at all of reconciling Great Britain and the Colonies?

Visitors allowed him a little time to greet his

176

daughter, who flung her arms around his neck with sobs of joy. Now for the first time Ben met his son-in-law, Richard Bache, and his two grandsons, Benjamin and William.

Stooping over his namesake, he said in a voice that shook with an old sorrow, "You look like my little lost son, Francis." But he quickly turned a beaming smile on the family and said gaily, "Well, this is a fine welcome for the old truant! I hope to do nothing but enjoy myself amongst you."

Vain hope. Within twenty-four hours a group of men from the Pennsylvania Assembly called upon him. "Dr. Franklin," said the spokesman proudly, "I have the honor to report your election to the Second Continental Congress."

Two days later, while Franklin was talking with his daughter, bells began to ring from State House and churches. Sally sprang up and pushed her two boys to the window. "Look! Look, children! See the fine soldiers on their horses!"

"Listen!" cried little Benjamin. "A band is playing."

William asked, "Who are all those men behind the soldiers?"

Ben had got up from his armchair to look. "The delegates to the convention from the southern states are riding in," he said. "There will be another escort when the New England delegates arrive."

On May 10th Franklin set out for the State House. So many friends rushed up to greet him that the walk became a triumphal procession. As he entered the hall, he looked around curiously. Here were the leaders who had been so abused by members of the English Parliament. John Adams and Samuel Adams from Boston were welcomed by men from Virginia, Maryland, New York, and the Carolinas. One after another, delegates came up to shake hands with Franklin and say an admiring word or two.

After the brief meeting at which the president and secretary of Congress were chosen, Franklin saw a tall man in a corner of the room shaking hands with the members who pressed around him.

Wearing a uniform of buff and blue, he was a striking figure. All at once the man saw Franklin and walked toward him with a smile lighting his grave face.

"Ah, Mr. Washington!" said Ben warmly. "So many years ago I last saw you in uniform and now you wear it again. I hear you are drilling troops in Virginia and Maryland."

Washington bowed. "Yes, as Patrick Henry said last March in Richmond, 'The time for action is at hand.' God grant, Dr. Franklin, that resistance will show King George he must teach Parliament to be just."

Franklin thought, "This Virginian is not ready for separation from the mother country."

Men from New England, however, talked openly of independence. At a dinner attended by all the delegates at the City Tavern, Sam Adams said, "Why should we be slaves to the tyrant, England? We must cut ourselves off from those chains."

The question of independence was the last of the

181

many problems before the Congress. First of all, they had to change the Congress into a governing body for all the Colonies. Next they set at the task of defending the country against British troops.

In the midst of this discussion one day the President was called from the room. When he came back, his face was aglow with triumph. Rapping the desk for attention, he said, "Gentlemen, a messenger has just brought good news from the north. The Green Mountain Boys of Vermont, led by Captain Ethan Allen, have captured Fort Ticonderoga on Lake Champlain!"

There was a thunder of applause. This success made everyone hopeful that American soldiers could win battles.

Soon after this day of rejoicing John Adams, through a Maryland delegate, asked Congress to make George Washington General-in-Chief of the American army. Everyone voted for him. Shyly and modestly Washington accepted the post. He said he would take no pay, but only money for expenses. On the 23rd of June, with Congress and all Philadelphia cheering him, the General set out to take command of the troops camped at Cambridge near Boston.

Hardly had he gone when news of the battle of Bunker Hill burst upon the city. This was really war. Every delegate was shaken to the core. Yet each man felt new pride in his heart. It was a battle lost, but with what glory! New England farmer boys had held for hours the finest troops in Europe and made them pay dear for victory.

No one was more moved than Franklin. The picture of British guns mowing down American boys stirred deep rage in his heart. For weeks he had been hoping that some change in England would prevent a complete break. Now he made up his mind that America must go on alone. With this certainty he felt he must see his son William. Surely even the Royal Governor of New Jersey would be compelled to abandon England and his post now. Hopefully he set out for a visit at his son's home.

When he returned, his daughter cried out at sight

of him, "Father, what has happened? Are you ill?"

"Yes, Sally, not in body, but in mind." He sank heavily into an armchair. "It's William. He thinks the Colonies are wrong to fight. He believes England is within her rights and means to remain a loyal servant of the King. Nothing I could say moved him. Oh, Sally, I've lost my son. Our ways have parted for good and all."

8

No one but Sally knew how much Franklin suffered over his son's failure to join the American struggle. He hid his feelings under the mountain of work piled on him. His daughter understood that this was best for him. She never tried to hold him back or tell him he was too old for dangerously hard trips.

Of course she was really glad when Congress sent him off to Cambridge in August. She knew he would see his sister and old friends.

"Tell General Washington," she laughed as she bade her father good-by, "that if you help organize the army, he'll surely chase out the British."

Sally was not in the least surprised to see her father come home from the trip looking far younger and gayer. "I'll wager you have been seeing some pretty young ladies," she teased, and rejoiced to hear his jolly laughter once more.

About some of Ben's other expeditions Sally worried in silence. It was an anxious moment when he rode away to Carlisle on a peace mission to the Indians. Still worse was his journey in the early spring of 1776 into Canada. Congress sent a commission to win sympathy for the Americans from the Canadian French. Franklin came back utterly exhausted from that cold, snowy, and vain journey.

Very meekly he obeyed his daughter's command to go at once to bed. But when she followed the Negro maid who carried his supper tray, she found him in dressing gown and slippers, hard at work on the papers heaped upon his desk. "Well, Sally," he replied to her scolding, "it isn't my head that's tired. And such as it is, the country seems to need it."

186

Franklin had again been made postmaster general for the Colonies. It was a big work to take the service over from the British Government. He had promptly appointed his son-in-law head of Philadelphia's post office and found him a great help.

Of all the many committees to which he was appointed, the most important was the Committee on Safety. He planned many new tools of war, and helped invent a huge barrier flung across the river to prevent British ships from coming within gun range of Philadelphia. Washington's very success in chasing the British out of Boston had brought the enemy nearer Philadelphia. Most of the troops landed in New York. A British fleet was expected soon. Washington was moving his army down to try to defend the city. If he failed, Philadelphia would probably be the next city attacked.

For weeks Franklin was too ill with gout to attend Congress. But he kept in touch with the leaders. They had given him a secret mission to write his friends in France, asking whether that country might give aid to America. Hints and rumors of

French interest in the struggle against England had excited hope. Early in the spring of '76, a man named Silas Deane was sent to France to report on the situation.

Meanwhile Congress was working toward the announcement of a final break with England. Each Colony had to vote on the matter. By April, eight Colonies were in favor of separation. Then a Congressional Committee was appointed to draw up for the whole country a statement of the reasons why independence was necessary and right. John Adams, Benjamin Franklin, and that brilliant young Virginian, Thomas Jefferson, were chosen for the task.

Adams came to Franklin's house one day to consult him. He was a man in his early forties, a lawyer and a great patriot. "Dr. Franklin," said he in his stiff and starchy way, "I have told Mr. Jefferson he ought to make a draft of this statement of independence. He writes very well and has great influence in the Colonies. We can edit the piece when it is set down. Is that agreeable to you?"

188

Ben smiled broadly. "Indeed, yes, Mr. Adams. I cannot think of a more thankless task than to write something to please a large number of people. Let young Jefferson do it and good luck to him!"

On July 4th, 1776, the vote on the finished work was taken. Ben limped to the State House for the great occasion. The delegates from New York would not vote. But the twelve other Colonies voted all together for separation and for Jefferson's statement. It was a long time before a copy of the document was ready, but at last each delegate signed the historic paper known as the Declaration of Independence. Benjamin Franklin's signature had a triumphant flourish. A few days after the vote was taken there was a thrilling ceremony at the State House. The Declaration was read from the balcony and the old bell rang out the tremendous news for all the world to hear.

Franklin, who had taken his little grandson to the square, bent down to say, "Remember this day, Benny. A new nation is born—God bless it!"

Some two months later, the household on Market Street was brimming with excitement. Richard Bache brought in a packet of mail from Europe and in it was a letter from one of Ben's powerful friends in Paris. Ben tore it open and read it as fast as he could translate. At the end of it he gave such a shout that Richard and Sally came running.

"Good news! Great news!" cried Ben. "My friend says the French people are positively aching to help us beat England. He thinks the government could be persuaded to give real aid. Where's my hat? Where's my stick? I must take this letter to Congress at once."

Leaders of Congress were also excited over the letter. It urged them to an important act. They decided to send a commission to Paris with full power to work out an alliance with France. Thomas Jefferson and Benjamin Franklin were chosen to go over and work with Silas Deane.

When Franklin came before the special committee of Congress to give his answer to the proposal, he looked at them with a droll smile. "Well, gentle-

192

men, I am old and good for nothing, but, as the storekeepers say of their remnants of cloth, I am but a fag end and you may have me for what you please."

Everyone agreed that the sooner the commission started, the better. The moment Franklin reached home he told the news to the family and made them promise never to say a word about the mission.

Sally listened, torn between pride and terrible anxiety. She feared she might never see her old father again. Of this she said nothing. She only asked him how he himself felt about going to France.

"Scared," he replied, laughing, "but glad to try to be useful."

He told Richard Bache that he would appoint him deputy postmaster in his absence and also announced that he was going to take William's son, Temple Franklin, with him. He meant to rescue the boy from royalist influences. In haste he set about his preparations. A thousand things had to be left shipshape before he sailed.

Early in October Franklin had word that Jefferson had refused to go to France because of his wife's illness. To fill his place, Congress was sending Arthur Lee, the American agent who had written letters hostile to Franklin when both men had been in London years before. Franklin was dashed not to have Jefferson as a traveling companion.

One morning he called his daughter into his room, looked at her with pleading eyes, and said, "Sally, I'm going to ask you the greatest favor of my life. It's a lonely business, this going off far from all I love. Could you, would you let me take little Benjamin with me?"

"What!" Sally could hardly believe her ears. Take a child of seven to a foreign country? Risk capture by the British on the high seas? At thought of parting with her adored little boy, a stab of pain shot through her. For a moment she stood in silent revolt. Then a wave of tender compassion for her father swept everything else away. "Take him, Father!" she said.

This time Franklin left Philadelphia with no

crowd to see him off, no cheers of farewell. He went in secret. With his two grandsons he boarded a ship lying stealthily in the Delaware River below Philadelphia.

As the vessel waited for a favorable wind, he sat with the captain over a glass of port, talking of the war. It had gone badly for two months. Defeated around New York, Washington had begun his retreat across New Jersey. His men were deserting by the hundreds. It was a dark moment.

"We can bear such bad times," said the captain, "if only the British don't succeed in getting control of the Hudson River and cutting off New England or capturing Washington's army."

"That they won't do!" said Franklin firmly. "He's too good a fox to be trapped."

When the ship began to slide down the river, Ben went to his cabin. In the light of the swinging lantern he bent over the bunk to look at little Ben. Tucking in a blanket, he stooped to kiss the round cheek flushed with sleep. If anything happened to the child, he would never forgive himself!

Straightening up, he went to the porthole and sniffed the salt air. Off for France! Well, somehow he thought it was going to be fun.

Thirty-three days later the coast of France came in sight. Franklin stood on deck between his two excited boys. The three of them were to land that day with their hand luggage and go on to Nantes by coach. This was a town on a big river.

Temple Franklin gently shifted the weight of the old man who clung to his arm. "Grandfather," he asked, "how do you feel?"

"Oh, I can hardly stand on my two pins. Every bone aches. But never mind! We've come across the sea in safety and in no time at all I'll be speaking my bad French and drinking lovely wines."

Little Benjamin had turned to stare at the bulky figure beside him. "Grandfather, why did you throw away your wig? You look odd without it in your fur cap."

"I threw it away because I did not need the thing any longer. We're going to a country where liberty and simplicity are in fashion, at least for others.

196

You'll see, boy. The French will like my fur hat and even my spectacles."

Ben was right. The moment they reached Nantes he began to hold court. Visitors flocked to see him. Ladies loved his peaked fur hat so much that they began arranging their hair as high as possible and called the arrangement *à la Franklin*. Ben was promptly given a dinner and a ball. All these flatteries refreshed him and he hated to tear himself away. On the 20th of December, escorted by Silas Deane, who drove out to meet him, Franklin reached Paris.

"Dr. Franklin," said Deane as they bounced along in the big carriage, "news of your coming has blown through Paris like the wind. The journals foretell your arrival and people are wild with joy. They seem to love America here, and you, of course, are an old friend."

Franklin was watching tall Temple and little Benny crane their necks out of the coach window for a first glimpse of the city. "And what about the King's minister?" he asked.

Deane frowned. "He had arranged to send arms and ammunition to America in secret, as you know. But the English ambassador got wind of it and the government had to stop the shipments. The government is worried over the bad news of our war and fears we might be beaten."

Franklin nodded calmly. "Yes, France wants peace. I saw that at Nantes. We'll go slowly with our plans."

But there was nothing slow about the way Parisians welcomed him. Crowds followed his carriage. Visitors crowded his hotel. The scientists he had met before came to pay their respects. Artists made engravings of his portrait and sold them like sugar cakes. In restaurants and at parties people asked one another, "Have you seen the Dr. Franklin? His fur hat, isn't it adorable?" Whoever talked with him went away saying, "Franklin is the true American, simple, natural, and grand."

A week after reaching the capital Franklin drove with Deane out to the royal palace about eleven miles southwest of Paris. There he was presented to the King's minister. Seated in the elegant reception room on a chair covered with tapestry, Ben listened to the Frenchman's polite talk and studied him closely. A large sum of money was to be loaned to America at once, but that was all the minister could promise at the moment.

Ben thought to himself, "This is a clever fellow. He really wants to help us, but doesn't dare get France into a war yet. He's waiting for a chance to bring a plan of alliance before the King. I'll not press him for action. I can play a waiting game, too."

For nearly two months Ben gave himself up to meeting great Parisians—nobles, bankers, people near the King. His fame as a scientist and writer, his humor and gaiety, even his dignified silence, made him very popular.

In his quiet way he made it plain that he was enjoying everything. No evidence of fine French taste was lost upon him. When he dined one evening with a great duke of the realm, his eyes, a gesture, and a word or two told his host how much he ad-

199

mired the beautiful drawing room. Behind his homely spectacles his eyes took in with relish the polished floors and thick, glowing rugs, the gilded chairs placed under magnificent portraits, the gleam, under the candelabra, of handsome bookbindings, porcelain ornaments, and tables of finest grain.

Well he knew that in his plain velvet suit and fur hat he made an odd contrast with the gorgeous company. But the ardor with which they gathered about him assured him that it was a contrast that pleased them. He noticed their delight when he murmured a word of praise at dinner for the truffles and ices and the marvelous concoctions of meat and fish.

The duke, who was a great lover of political freedom, asked his guest of honor eager questions about the constitutions of the American states. Helped out by both the ladies and gentlemen seated near him, Franklin made slow answers. But these proved how well he knew his country, how proud he was of its progress in self-government.

"Dr. Franklin," said the duke, "it would be a splendid thing for Frenchmen to study these American state constitutions. I should like to get them, translate them into French, and have them published here. Would you be so generous as to help me?"

"With all my heart, Monsieur le Duc," replied Franklin eagerly.

He was happy to fan the feeling of Frenchmen that America was the land of liberty. It was plain to him that he seemed to stand for his country and for the freedom they loved. But he did not want to keep up a gay life in Paris. He wanted to behave like the simple man people wanted him to be.

Just then he had an invitation from a rich merchant, a warm friend of America. He had a big house and gardens in an outlying part of Paris called Passy.

"Dr. Franklin," said he, "on my place in Passy stands a villa which I should be honored to have you use. It is nothing, but it is comfortable and will give you more privacy than an hotel."

Franklin accepted the gift at once. From the first, he was enchanted with the place. His villa stood at the end of a magnificent garden shaded by fine trees. Passy was like a big park where lovely villas and lawns stretched for miles. When the neighbors came to call, Ben found them delightful.

The first thing he did was to place little Benjamin in a good boarding school near by. As for Temple, he trained the youth to copy his letters and serve as his secretary. Each morning Franklin wrote to Congressional leaders, to Sally, to friends in France, England, and America, and to strangers who had written to ask him favors.

Almost every evening he dined out with friends or invited them to dine with him. One charming Frenchwoman after another craved his company, and their playful, flattering ways made him feel young and gay. He needed these good times for he worked hard. Many afternoons were spent in talking over problems with Silas Deane and Arthur Lee.

"I am at my wit's end," said Deane, "about the

men who wish to go to America. Most of them are fortune hunters. All of them want to be made officers in the American army with pay."

"Not the young Marquis I've heard so much about—not Lafayette!" said Franklin.

Deane smiled at the thought of the romantic young man. "No. He bought his own ship and went at his own expense. He is a true idealist. All his relatives tried to stop him, but go he would. I hope General Washington will receive him well."

"Yes," said Franklin, "he could help our cause. His wife's family is one of the most powerful in France. If he wins them over to friendship with America, they would influence King Louis."

Franklin met Lafayette's lovely young wife and her parents at their great house in Paris. Hurt as they were by the secret departure of the Marquis, they wanted to help him. They gave Franklin a sum of money to be sent to America and placed in the hands of some understanding person who would dole it out to Lafayette as he needed it.

Franklin smiled and bowed. "To General Washington, in short," said he. Promptly he sent the money with a letter recommending the young man to Washington as a valuable friend from every standpoint.

In France, as in London, Franklin wrote about his country for newspapers and magazines. He told the French how productive it was, how hard the farmers and pioneers worked, how impossible it was for the British to conquer a people who loved freedom so much. Washington's capture of the Hessians at Trenton on Christmas Eve and his success at Princeton gave proof of Franklin's statements.

Then came news which made the American agents anxious. General Burgoyne had landed a big army at Quebec and was marching it south in two sections.

"The British," said Arthur Lee, "mean to capture all the country around the Hudson River and cut off New England. If they succeed, it will be a death blow to us."

All summer Franklin waited for news. There

was none about Burgoyne. Dispatches reported only that Washington was retreating into Pennsylvania and that the British Admiral was sailing up the Delaware River.

When Benjamin Bache came for Sunday dinner, he would ask in a scared tone, "Grandfather, have the British taken Philadelphia? They wouldn't hurt Father and Mother, would they?"

Franklin told him that letters from his mother said the whole family had moved to the country. But not until December 3rd was he certain what had happened to the city. Word came that day from Paris that a special messenger from Congress had landed and was coming to see him. In an hour's time the house was full of neighbors and friends, eager to hear the news. Into the courtyard rattled a carriage. Out of it sprang a smiling young man.

Franklin stood in the hall. He was trembling with excitement. "Sir, is Philadelphia taken?" he cried.

"Yes, sir, but I have greater news than that! General Burgoyne has surrendered, and the entire

British Army of the North has been made prisoner."

Ah, what a moment! Men cheered. Ladies flung their arms about Franklin. Young men kicked their heels in a dance of joy. Wine was called for and toasts were drunk to the United States of America! One man jumped into his carriage and hurried off to be the first to tell the news in Paris. Franklin, Lee, and Deane sat up till morning writing bulletins to send to the French minister and newspapers and leading men in all parts of France.

At dawn Franklin, pale and tired, with hair hanging limp, sat down for coffee with Silas Deane. They spoke of their relief that Philadelphia had not been shelled with cannon. The British had quietly settled there for the winter, to keep watch on Washington's camp of starving, freezing soldiers at Valley Forge. Congress had fled to another town, but citizens were treated politely.

Franklin set down his cup, went to stand by the fire, and cried, "Now our friend at court will act. Surely King Louis will make a public alliance with us!"

At once he set to work to bring this about. He pretended to be trying for peace with England. There were always English spies and agents in Paris. Franklin talked with some of them, wrote letters to important men in London, and asked on what terms the British would stop fighting. He soon found out that the English Government, even King George, wanted peace, but would not grant independence to America. These interviews Franklin reported to the French minister.

But the minister had not been slow to act. Three days after the news of Burgoyne's surrender reached him, he sent an important man to Franklin to say that now the King was ready to consider an alliance with the United States. The American agents set down the conditions of the alliance and Temple Franklin took the paper to the minister. Four days passed. Then the three agents had a secret meeting with the minister of King Louis.

The Frenchman was radiant. "Gentlemen, His Majesty is to consult our ally, Spain. Then, I believe, it is certain he will announce an alliance on your terms with the United States of America."

Franklin feared delay. But the French were alarmed because the English kept on trying to make peace terms with Franklin. King Louis' minister hastened to work out a treaty and send it to Passy for approval by the Americans. After certain points were settled, both parties agreed. A trade treaty and a political treaty were ready to be signed.

March 20th, 1778, was set for the King to receive the agents at his palace. At that time he was to announce the French-American Alliance. All Passy was excited. Temple Franklin and Benjamin Bache could talk of nothing else.

"Of course, Grandfather," said Temple, "you are going to wear a wig."

But when everyone gathered in the Passy drawing room on the great day, the boys saw that Franklin's white hair was carefully combed over his shoulders. He looked as different as possible from Deane and Lee, who were in full court dress of satin, laces, swords, and curled wigs. Franklin wore no sword. The dazzlingly white ruffles at throat and wrists were of plainest lawn and under his arm he carried a white hat.

"Grandfather, that old suit!" groaned Temple. "It's too tight for you. Why did you search that out of your traveling box?"

Benjamin stepped to the long mirror hung on the drawing-room wall and smiled at the plump figure which met his gaze. He had unearthed the same suit of figured Manchester velvet which he had worn on the day the British Crown prosecutor held him up to scorn. It seemed to him a charming idea to put on that costume for the ceremony of alliance with Britain's foe.

Turning back to his companions, Ben said, "This suit is my little joke." His lips curved with mischief.

Temple, seeing the expression of disdain on Lee's face, said crossly, "Joke it is, sir, but what does it mean?"

Ben answered with a chuckle, "I fancy there will be plenty of English spies at the palace today who will understand my joke very well."

In this he was quite correct. News that Franklin had appeared in that velvet suit sped to London and the King's ministers said with worried frowns, "He will never forgive us."

Upon the French crowds gathered in front of the palace to salute the American commissioners, Franklin's appearance had quite a different effect. People gasped in admiration at the dignified simplicity of this famous American. He brought a Quaker touch to the splendor of the scene.

Drums were beating. Flags were flying. Troops in gorgeous uniforms were presenting arms. Franklin walked up the palace steps with tears of joy burning his eyelids. France, the great and magnificent, was welcoming as a friend the youngest nation on earth!

Through the palace halls, jammed with nobles, fine ladies, professors, and diplomats, they walked. At last the minister led them to a small room hung with beautiful paintings. There sat the King. He was a fat, serious-looking young man. Smiling, he held out his hand to Franklin and nodded to the other two Americans.

"Gentlemen," said he, "assure Congress of my friendship. I hope this will be for the good of the two nations." Then he added a word of praise for the American agents.

In halting French Franklin thanked King Louis. "Your Majesty may count on the gratitude of Congress," he said.

After they left the King, the three men were taken to dinner in the minister's private apartment. They toasted the alliance in the finest French wine. Later in a huge drawing room of the palace they were presented to Queen Marie Antoinette and a company of court ladies and gentlemen. The young queen was beautiful and impressive, with her high-piled, powdered hair, her jewels, the gleaming gown adorning her slender figure. With every air of wishing to please him, she talked a long time with Franklin.

Dazzled and triumphant, Franklin at last sank into a corner of his coach and started back to Passy.

"What a day!" he murmured to Deane. "History has been made and a war has been won by the signing of this treaty. Oh, bless me, how my poor gouty feet hurt!"

9

Franklin knew the war had not actually been won yet, but neither he nor the men in the French government thought it would last long. What troubled them all most was the matter of expense. Congress had no funds but paper money. To pay soldiers and buy supplies the leaders needed millions in cash from France. But now that France was in the war, too, she had to spend large sums on troops and ships. Every time Franklin asked for a new loan from the minister, he felt he was draining blood from France.

"These bills from America are appalling," he

said to Temple. "Congress draws on loans from France before I've had a chance to secure them."

All his tasks were made harder because of Arthur Lee's jealousy. For a year now Lee had been writing Congress harsh reports of Franklin. He also accused Silas Deane of making money from the purchase of French supplies. Deane went back to America, but was never able to make Congress believe in his innocence.

In April, 1778, John Adams was sent over as first ambassador to France. Franklin gave him rooms in his villa and warmly welcomed John Quincy Adams, aged ten, who had arrived with his father.

"It is a fine thing you came, Johnny," said Franklin. "My grandson will be delighted to have another boy around. I must show you the printing press I've set up here, but you'll like even better the little cakes my cook makes."

John Quincy was at once placed in the same school with Benjamin Bache, and the two boys spent every Sunday at Franklin's villa. He took them swimming in the Seine and played with them in the garden. On hot afternoons they ate ices on the terrace and listened to Franklin's stories.

It was a pity that Johnny's father did not share his son's liking for Franklin. Adams thought his way of doing business careless, and reported to Congress that the household at Passy was extravagant. But Adams himself did not get on very well with the French minister. Finally the minister was so annoyed with the New Englander's preachy ways that he said he would only do business with Franklin. Since Adams always thought he was in the right, he began to hate his fellow American.

Yet Adams had to watch Franklin courted by distinguished people and heaped with honors. That year at a meeting of the famous scientific society of France, Franklin was presented to one of the greatest Frenchmen who ever lived—Voltaire. Everyone present cheered these two men who had done so much for human liberty.

One Sunday in June, Franklin looked around the dinner table, smiled at Johnny and Benny, and said, "I think we ought to give a party to celebrate the Fourth of July."

The boys were delighted. Even John Adams thought it would be a good idea. They invited all the neighbors and all the Americans in Paris. There were flowers on the table. American and French flags fluttered in the garden, and toasts were drunk to France and America. Johnny and Benny had all the cakes and ices they could eat, and everyone had a glorious time.

Dinner parties, gay hours with the children, and evenings of playing chess with one of his neighbors kept Ben cheerful in the midst of his tiresome duties. He was always working on the exchange of American prisoners for British prisoners. When American sea captains captured English ships and brought them into French ports, he had to settle rewards and divide spoils. It was no easy matter to take up all the many problems of the war with the French minister without offending Adams still further.

Ben threw off weariness and remained serene by

216

enjoying himself when he could. Finding that the Frenchwomen whom he knew best loved his wit, he sometimes printed for them on his press verses and funny little tales. From the depths of himself he drew up a kind of merry calm. And it was this expression which a great French sculptor caught in a portrait bust he modeled of Franklin that year.

Toward the end of it, word came that Congress was calling John Adams home and appointing Franklin ambassador in his place. In spite of jealous enemies who had tried to make members of Congress distrust him, Ben Franklin was chosen for the post he had so well earned. It made him very happy.

One morning in February, 1779, a servant knocked at Ben's study door. He was busy writing a report to Congress. Temple was filing copies of letters in the way John Adams had demanded. But the servant's message put an end to work. Both the Franklins hurried downstairs to welcome the visitor waiting in the drawing room.

A tall young man in a splendid uniform sprang

to his feet at sight of them. In spite of a forehead slanting straight back from a long, pointed nose, he had a most attractive air.

Striding forward, he cried in strongly accented English, "At last I meet you, the Dr. Franklin of such world fame!"

Beaming with pleasure, Franklin said, "And at last I meet the good friend of the United States, the Marquis de Lafayette."

He was back in France after the terrible winter of Valley Forge, after a gallant campaign in which he had been wounded. His family had welcomed him with pride, and all Paris was ringing with his glory.

"My first affair, Monsieur the doctor," said Lafayette, opening his dispatch case, "is to present you with papers from Congress sealing your appointment as ambassador to France. It is an honor, dear Doctor, to be the messenger."

For hours Lafayette and Franklin talked of the war, of the French alliance, and of Washington, whom the young French officer adored. The Marquis had already paid his respects to the French ministers. They were somewhat discouraged by lack of success in the American war. The French fleet sent over the year before had been bottled up by the English and had given no aid at all.

"General Washington, that great man," said Lafayette, "keeps the enemy from conquering. But to win he must have help. France must send battleships which will do battle. I have told His Majesty this."

Franklin was at once reminded of John Paul Jones. This resolute seaman was in Paris, asking for a ship. He wanted to raid the British coast and sink British supply boats.

"I've told the young man to see you," said Franklin. "I believe in him. He is brave and eager to help and he knows the sea. I beg you, Marquis, to use your influence at court to get him an armed vessel."

Lafayette promised to do so. From that day on the Marquis counted himself one of Franklin's devoted friends. He called at Passy when he could and wrote Ben about his interviews at the palace and his plans. The warmth in the hearts of both men, their admiration for George Washington, and their love of America drew them close together. Lafayette admired Franklin's genius and his way of finding life fascinating no matter what happened. Ben thought the romantic young Frenchman had a grace which matched his enthusiasm and sincerity.

"What a comfort he must have been to Washington," Ben said to John Adams.

When the time came for Adams to leave, Franklin felt sad at saying good-by to little Johnny. The boy wrote Ben a letter just before boarding the ship with his father, and signed it, "Your affectionate friend."

On March 23rd, Franklin went to present himself at court as the new ambassador from the United States. King Louis received him graciously, and the ministers were pleased that at last the American they trusted most had been given the office. Franklin paid his respects to all the royal

family and came home with such swollen feet that
he could hardly move for a week.

Now that he was in sole command of American
affairs in France, they went peaceably again. But
he missed little Benjamin, who was now in school
in Switzerland. How he wished the boy had been
with him to share the news which brightened the
September skies over Passy! John Paul Jones was
the hero. He had sailed out in an old tub of a ship
given him by the French. He had called it the
Bonhomme Richard—Good Fellow Richard—in
honor of Franklin's famous character, Poor Richard.

First Paul Jones had gone up and down the
coast of Scotland, Ireland, and Northern England
to destroy shipping. Then he had won a glorious
battle with an English armed vessel and brought it
into a French port. All France was thrilled. It was
a great day for Passy when the hero came to call
on the ambassador.

The old countryman who sold Franklin wood
hung about for a glimpse of the captain. He stam-

mered out in excitement, "Ah, Monsieur the doctor, you Americans can fight on sea as well as on land!"

Lafayette was going back to America early in 1780. He was taking big news to Washington. A French fleet and armed force were sailing for America. They were sorely needed. The English were doing battle in the south now and were winning everywhere. To cheer Washington in this grim period, Franklin wrote him that everyone in Europe was applauding him as "one of the greatest captains of our age." Franklin and Lafayette agreed that with enough French aid the great captain would be victorious.

As 1781 began, this seemed no vain hope. American generals were beginning to wear down the British troops in the Carolinas. By summer Lafayette was leading the enemy a chase in Virginia.

These events added to the pleasure Franklin took that summer in a country festival. It was given in his honor by a countess at her fine estate. The whole company walked half a mile to escort

224

him to the house and chanted verses written for the occasion.

Late in the autumn arrived news which set France aflame with joy. The British had met a stunning defeat. American land forces had penned up the English army in Yorktown, Virginia. Two French fleets beat off the British fleet as it hurried to the rescue. There was nothing for the British general to do but surrender with all his men.

From then on, England, France, and America began to talk about making peace. Lafayette returned and came out to Passy to tell his friend about the magnificent victory at Yorktown. The Marquis thought the English were sick and tired of the war.

"Yes," said Franklin, "I hear that from my friends in England who have never approved of the course taken by King George. I am told that the King's ministers are out of office. Men I knew who were always friendly to America now head the government. They have begun to make signals to me across the Channel."

By this he meant that one British agent after another was sent over to talk with Franklin. What terms would America accept? He politely refused to give a definite answer. Instead, he suggested that the British Government make an offer of peace. Every interview was frankly reported by Franklin to the French minister.

John Adams was again in Paris. He was commissioned to help Franklin work out a treaty of peace. This time Mrs. Adams came with her husband. When Franklin introduced her to his French friends, she was shocked at the gaiety of the ladies of Passy.

Next arrived John Jay, an excellent lawyer from New York. He also was a member of the peace commission. Month after month, discussions and conferences went on.

Making the peace was no simple matter. France wanted certain rewards for her share in the victory. England was determined to give up as little as possible and to protect those Americans who had been loyal to the British. King George fought furiously against granting American independence. But the United States, on the other hand, stated that England must admit their independence even before the treaty was drawn up. Moreover, Congress insisted that England give up all claim to lands south of the border of Canada down to Florida and Louisiana, and as far west as the Mississippi River.

One day as the three Americans sat in Franklin's study arguing about the latest English report, John Jay said, "Doesn't it seem strange that while we sit here talking about peace, Washington still has to hold his army together to watch the British in New York?"

"Yes," said Adams, "and battles still go on in the south. But the states have stopped worrying about the war and it is harder than ever to get people to vote the money to finish it."

"Money!" groaned Franklin. "It is unbearable to think of having to ask for another French loan. I thank Heaven that Lafayette is here to help explain our need for it."

227

Nevertheless, France sent a substantial sum to America, not as a loan, but as a gift.

On into 1783 dragged the conferences. Franklin was delighted that a new excitement was sweeping through France to give everyone a change. In a big city toward the southeast of France a man had made an interesting experiment. He had sent up a huge balloon filled with hot air. At once a scientist in Paris made a bigger, better balloon and filled it with gas. On the day he sent it up an enormous crowd gathered to watch. Franklin drove in from Passy to see the great event.

A cannon was fired. The balloon ropes were untied. "Ah!" sighed thousands of voices. "There it goes into the sky!"

Beside Franklin stood a man he knew in the Society of Scientists. Turning with a sniff, the man said, "But what use is a balloon?"

Franklin stared at him. He thought of all his own simple experiments which became important, all the attempts men had made through the ages to conquer the forces of earth, sea, and sky. How

228

could anyone say what would happen in the future from this idea of the balloon? If it proved that something heavier than air could float in air, men might some day travel through the clouds.

With gentle sarcasm he replied to the scientist, "Well, Monsieur, what is the use of a new-born baby?"

When John Jay's wife heard somebody repeat Ben's remark, she laughed delightedly. The Jays were staying at Franklin's villa and their two-week-old baby was with them. Every day Ben would take the baby in his arms and smile coaxingly. Soon the little thing would stop crying and seemed content whenever he picked her up.

"It's charming to have an infant here," Ben said to Mrs. Jay. "She makes me forget how serious I am always supposed to be."

At last on September 3rd, 1783, two peace treaties were signed. First the Americans went to the hotel where the British agents were staying and there signed the papers. The final treaty, however, had to be accepted by Congress. On the same day the treaty between England and France was signed.

Peace! Washington could disband his army and return to his plantation in Virginia. The tired, disgusted British troops could sail back to England. And patient, courteous Franklin could bow to the door the American commissioners and wish them a safe voyage home.

Ben sighed happily to Temple, "Now I'll have time to take up some scientific studies again. And also to see my friends."

Temple sighed, not so happily, that for his part he would miss all the excitement. Ben looked at him anxiously. He had tried his best, without success, to persuade Congress to give his grandson some appointment. It was a pity that the good-looking youth had neither special training nor ambition for anything but having a good time. "I've spoiled him," thought Franklin, and made up his mind then and there to have Benjamin taught the printing trade.

Ben's hope of enjoying himself was blurred by

illness. Even on his sick bed, however, he wrote some witty pieces and charming letters. As soon as he was better, he served on a scientific commission appointed by King Louis. And, sick or well, he kept on with his many duties as ambassador to France. Chief of these was writing treaties with European countries.

In the summer of 1784 Thomas Jefferson was sent over to help with that work. It was a warm, misty day when he first went to dine with Franklin at Passy. There were a number of French people at the noon dinner. But later, over coffee, the two Americans sat alone on the terrace, sniffing the fragrance of mignonette wafted from the garden on the soft air. Benjamin looked at his companion with approval because his thick sandy hair was not covered by a wig. He was certain that the young man's simple elegance would delight the French.

"I am relieved, Dr. Franklin," Jefferson said, "to find you able to be about again. Your illness disturbed us all."

Franklin turned his smiling eyes from his friend

231

to the long lanes of clipped linden trees which framed the formal gardens. "It sometimes comes over me that I am getting old. I really cannot see unless I wear spectacles all the time. And look, Mr. Jefferson, at the cunning thing I have devised."

Taking off his spectacles, he handed them to his companion. "I grew so tired," he went on, "of constantly taking off my reading spectacles and putting on my spectacles for seeing things at a distance, and then doing the reverse, that I thought of this way of relieving myself of trouble. See? I have divided the glass in two within the same frame. The lower half of the glass is for reading and the upper half is for seeing things at a distance."

Jefferson had been turning over the spectacles in his long, sensitive fingers. "This is a remarkable invention!" he cried with warm admiration. "Bifocal spectacles! I'm sure, sir, that this kind of lens will be copied from now on. It is like you, Dr. Franklin, to put to use what you have thought out."

232

After he had been in Paris only a short time Jefferson wrote:

"I find more respect and veneration attached to the character of Dr. Franklin in France than to that of any other person, foreign or native."

Indeed, through his lightning rods, the French translation of "Poor Richard," and his years of work in France, Franklin's name was known in the most remote villages. Yet his own knowledge of the French people was limited to charming, learned, wealthy individuals. He had no notion of the violent change which was coming in France.

At the clubs to which he belonged the young nobles who gathered about him seemed to him quite able to bring about better things for France in a peaceful way. They spoke out boldly for freedom of the press and of religion. In government they wanted an elected congress to represent the nation. Ben's life in serene Passy and the luxurious court gave him no picture of the wretched, hungry families in city and country. He did not know that France was bankrupt. Nor could he guess at the angry discontent boiling under the delightful surface of French life.

Franklin enjoyed every hour he spent with Thomas Jefferson. It was interesting to work with a man whose quick, keen brain was matched by his warm, human sympathies. Luncheon at Passy, when Ben was well enough to come to the table, became a feast of good fellowship. For the Virginian not only savored the exquisitely seasoned stew, called *pot-au-feu*, and the croquettes and custards and delicate wines, but, unlike John Adams, he also delighted in the company of abbés and professors and of Ben's good neighbors. What stories they told! What laughter rang out!

Yet there was a stronger reason why Franklin had welcomed Jefferson's coming. He saw in the brilliant young man a means of laying down the burden of his duties. He knew the cultured, free-thinking Virginian would understand France and serve American interests well.

Ever since his severe illness, Franklin had asked Congress for leave to return to America. At last permission came and he prepared to depart. Temple Franklin was too absorbed in packing his own clothes and fussing over his Angora cat to be much help. But Benjamin Bache worked day after day to get his grandfather's books and possessions properly boxed.

Messages of farewell poured in upon Franklin. From the King of France came a miniature of himself set in diamonds. All the ministers wrote him warm good-bys. To his friends at Passy he gave little gifts to comfort their sorrow at parting from him. He shared that sorrow, but his longing to see his daughter and his country had become overwhelming.

"If I wait any longer," he said to Jefferson, "I might not live to get there."

To make his journey to the coast easier, the French government sent him the Queen's litter, a kind of bed on wheels, drawn by mules. Propped on cushions, Ben waved good-by to his weeping

235

friends at Passy and to the crowds who lined the road. Everywhere the royal litter stopped, friends gathered to welcome and entertain the departing ambassador.

"Just think, Benny," he said to his grandson, "I have been in France nine years, nine happy years. Of all nations in the world, the French know best how to make themselves beloved by strangers."

"You will miss France, Grandfather," said Benny.

"Yes," he said thoughtfully, "but America is home."

10

Several times during the journey across France to the packet boat Benny anxiously asked Temple, "Do you really think Grandfather will live to get home?"

On the 4th of September, as the ship tacked its way up the Delaware River, Temple reminded his cousin of those fears. All the passengers were out on deck and the two boys stood side by side, watching the river craft and the changing line of the shore.

"Look at Grandfather now!" laughed Temple. "He hasn't even been seasick."

Franklin, in dark suit and snowy frilled shirt, was at the rail. He was gazing eagerly at the distant spires and rooftops of Philadelphia. Although somewhat thinner and a little pale, he had an air of remarkable vigor. Suddenly he turned toward his grandsons and lifted his voice in a boyish shout.

"We're going to drop anchor soon!" With a half-amused, half-scornful glance at Temple, he added, "You'd better go below and get your cat."

Soon the ship's great sails were furled and the anchor had hissed its way to the bottom. Already a large rowboat was speeding from the wharf across the strip of water. Franklin was the first to recognize the man in the stern.

"It's your father, Benny!" he exclaimed. "Good Richard Bache is coming to fetch us ashore."

Franklin was savoring each moment. When his son-in-law had scrambled to the deck, he greeted him with affection. Then he stood aside to watch Bache stare unbelievingly at the tall, broad-shouldered fellow who had come back in place of little Benny. After they were all seated in the boat and

238

the oarsmen had pushed off, he gave an amused chuckle.

"Well, Richard," said he, "I see I'm going to land at the Market Street wharf, just as I did sixty-two years ago."

For a moment memory handed him a clear picture of that rumpled, penniless youth, the runaway printer's apprentice. But cheers from the crowd on the wharf, the ringing of bells, and the boom of a cannon reminded him that an ambassador was being welcomed home from France. Soon he was looking into a multitude of faces, familiar old ones, smiling youngsters, curious strangers. In a chorus of cheers he reached his own door at last.

It was some time before the Bache family settled down to talk. Benny and Benjamin had to greet all the little Bache children whom they had never seen. Benjamin prowled around the house a little.

He said to Richard, "I think I'll have to build a new wing to hold all my books and the stuff I've brought from France."

When they sat down for tea, Sally turned from

eager talk with Benny to ask, "Father, how did you really stand the trip? I've been so anxious."

He merely replied, "Very well, my dear."

But his grandsons gave more details. "He was taking the temperature of the Gulf Stream every day," said Benny. "He was writing for hours and hours in his cabin," said Temple. "Yes, writing all sorts of things about how to make ships safe," added Benny.

Franklin laughed. "A sea voyage gives one time and peace for work. I've written a letter to a man in Vienna, which may have some general interest, on the causes and cure of smoky chimneys."

"I'm glad, sir, you had leisure on shipboard!" said Richard Bache. "For I'm sure you'll have none here."

That was, indeed, the truth. Beginning next day, there was a stream of callers for a week. Speeches of praise and welcome were made by members of the Pennsylvania Assembly, by university professors, by members of clubs and societies. Franklin always made a grateful, if brief, reply.

240

A few evenings after his arrival, he went to a meeting of his old fire company. He returned home to find Sally, fat, middle-aged, and comfortable, sitting before the stove, knitting a sock. With a sigh of content Ben sank into an armchair.

"Sally," said he, "there are only four men alive who joined the fire company when I founded it nearly fifty years ago."

"Did it make you feel lonely?" she asked gently.

"Oh, no. The sons of my old friends cheered me roundly when I said that at the next meeting I'd have my fire bucket and basket ready as usual."

Within a month Franklin was elected President of the Pennsylvania Assembly. He did not preside often at the sessions, but met with the Council to advise on plans. It was interesting to him to be in the swing of things again. Besides, his duties kept him from missing his boys so much. Temple finally decided to live on the farm his father had given him, and Benny was going to college.

Whenever young Ben came home, he was eager to get his grandfather's opinions of affairs in

America. They were in a state of confusion. The
Continental Congress still met, but it had no power
to make the states act. The debts it had piled up
during the war were huge, and the paper money it
issued was almost worthless. Dozens of serious
problems faced the new nation, yet there was no
trusted government to solve them.

Franklin never seemed worried about the general discontent. He said to his grandson, "Many
people speak to me and write to me about the need
of remaking the central government. That will
happen some day and things will right themselves."

"But, Grandfather, something ought to be done
soon! Just think how merchants have to pay tariffs
for things they buy in other states! And I never saw
such odd coins as those used here for money—
French sous, Spanish doubloons, English coins of
all sorts. We ought to have money of our own as
other nations do."

"Quite so." Franklin poured himself some min-
eral water which he had brought from France. "My
boy, when people get tired enough of annoying

things, they'll find a cure. The states will have to give Congress more power and give up a bit of their independence."

Attacks of pain and weakness often kept Franklin at home now. Then he would read for days and nights at a time, write letters to friends abroad and at home, and talk with companions of former days. When he felt better, he would go to small parties. He loved to watch young people dancing minuets and reels. He liked listening to music and enjoyed cribbage and other card games. Not only did he put a wing on his house to serve as a library, but built two other houses on his land.

Slowly out of his calm and busy life sprang new interest in the affairs of the nation. The gazettes were full of stories about a convention to be held in May, 1787, in Philadelphia. Delegates from every state were coming together to discuss how to make over the rickety old Congress and work out trade agreements. In March of that year, Franklin was elected with seven other men to represent Pennsylvania.

Robert Morris, the banker, was also a delegate. One day when Franklin was dining with him he said, "From hints and rumors, I gather that a number of delegates wish to sink the old Congress and launch an entirely new government."

Franklin of course had heard that, too. "Young James Madison is one who feels that way, I understand," said he. "I wonder if Mr. Jefferson has influenced his thought. 'Tis a pity Jefferson will not be here, and I'll wager John Adams would give up his post in England to come and argue everyone down."

Morris said he hoped to entertain George Washington during the convention. And on May 13th Franklin learned that the great man was arriving. From his window Ben watched a troop of light horse gallop from the city and return after some hours, escorting Washington's coach. Three days later the famous Virginian came to noon dinner at Franklin's house.

Washington took the soft wrinkled hand held out to him in both his own. Although each had

244

written the other, the two had not met since the beginning of the war in Boston. After their exchange of warm greetings Franklin asked about Lafayette's visit to America in '84.

At mention of his young friend's name, Washington looked sober. "There is great unrest in France," said he. "The country is bankrupt. The poor cannot be forced to pay any more taxes, and so far the rich have refused to vote money. I fear for the future in that country."

Talk then turned at once to the problems facing the convention. Deep in their hearts these two men knew they had had the widest experience and were therefore the most responsible for the spirit in which the tremendously important work was done.

After dinner Franklin showed his guest his new library. Washington, who had only a few books and most of those on farming, gasped at the sight of bookshelves running from floor to ceiling around three walls.

"How do you reach the volumes on the top shelf, Dr. Franklin?" he asked. Stretching his tall figure up on his toes to look, he added, "I see most of those are in French."

"Look at my handy helper," replied Ben, laughing. He picked up a wooden pole with a kind of claw at the end which could be opened and closed by a lever at the handle. In a twinkling Ben had whisked down a book written by Voltaire.

"And here's another useful thing for a library," said he. It was a kind of chair which could be turned into a small stepladder. Washington was charmed with these clever inventions.

The next time the two men met was at the opening of the convention on May 26th at the State House. Seven states were represented by twenty-nine men. Without waiting for the other delegates, the body at once elected Washington President of the Assembly. Slowly representatives from all the states but Rhode Island gathered in the fine old hall and set to work.

It was some time before the convention members agreed to form a new government. Most of them had not expected such a task. But several men had

plans for a national congress and point by point they were talked over.

Often when he was lame from gout Benjamin had himself carried in a litter to and from the State House. One afternoon when he came home for tea in the garden, Sally asked him, "What do you talk about all day, Father? Tell me what goes on."

He shook his head. "The meetings are absolutely secret, Sally. And since there is not a woman delegate amongst us, the secret is sure to be kept." And he laughed teasingly.

' All through the hot summer, fifty-five men built the new government like a house, brick by brick. Often there was fierce disagreement. Men from small states feared the power of big states. Some wanted the President to be almost like a king. Others were afraid to give him any power at all. But, little by little, the delegates stopped thinking of themselves as belonging to states and began to see that they were there to serve a nation.

Franklin followed everything with keen interest. But he was too feeble to make speeches. Now and then he wrote something and asked one of the younger men to read it to the Assembly. Once, when it seemed as if the clash of opinions would wreck all that had been accomplished, he rose to his feet.

"Mr. President," said he, "I propose that the convention shall adjourn for three days to afford time for more full, free study of the subject."

Everyone saw that this wise, experienced leader was alarmed to think of failure. Angry faces softened. Everyone voted to do as he said. When the convention opened three days later, an agreement was reached. Washington's patience and Franklin's feeling of brotherhood did much to hold the convention together.

At last on the 17th of September, 1787, the American Constitution was ready. When the final vote was called, Franklin arose, handed a written speech to another Pennsylvania delegate, and stood while it was read. The humor of it made the Assembly laugh. Its tolerance won over all who were hesitating.

At the end he said, "Thus I consent, sir, to this Constitution because I expect no better and because I am not sure that it is not the best." Then he asked that the vote be unanimous in favor of adoption and that everyone sign the Constitution.

His part in this mighty work for the nation was Franklin's last important service. True, he was again elected President of the Pennsylvania Assembly, but was seldom able to go to meetings. With breathless interest he followed the reports of the conventions held by each state to adopt the Constitution. When eleven states had voted for it, he was profoundly happy. And the choice of George Washington for the first President was his choice.

Only the news from France worried him. The riots and disorder in Paris, he thought, would be cured when the King called the national assembly to meet for the first time in one hundred and seventy-five years. But the storming of the Bastille shook his hope of peaceful change. He was troubled about his friends.

With what joy he welcomed Thomas Jefferson

one afternoon! Jefferson had come back to serve as Washington's Secretary of State and was on his way to join the government in New York. As soon as he stepped into the bedroom where the sick man lay propped on pillows, Franklin asked for news from France.

"What about our friends in Passy? And Lafayette?" He went on naming one after another.

Jefferson could report their safety and brought messages from many of them. Not for the world would the young man have chased away the happy smile on Franklin's face by speaking of his own fears of civil war in France. Instead, he changed the subject.

"I hear you have been writing again the story of your life, Dr. Franklin. That is good, indeed."

The long upper lip twisted with its old humor. "I cannot say much of that, sir. But I'll give you a sample of it." Thereupon he pressed upon his visitor as a farewell gift a sheaf of the manuscript.

So refreshed was Franklin by Jefferson's visit that a few days later he wrote a lively piece for the

Federal Gazette. In it he made an amusing attack on a stupid Southerner who said it was never the business of Congress to meddle with slavery.

Yes, Franklin would live, love his friends, work, defend the rights of man, and have fun in his own way so long as breath was in his body. No one was ever less afraid of death. On April 17th, 1790, at the age of eighty-four he slipped quietly over the edge of his long, rich life.

One of his young friends said that it was too bad Ben could not see his own funeral. It was a pageant of all his work for the city. Members of the fire companies, the hospital, library, and university, members of the Assembly and of a dozen societies, a company of militia—they were all there, walking to muffled bells under the flags set at half-mast, to do honor to their greatest citizen.

That procession was merely the beginning. In every part of the newborn United States, in England, France, and other countries of Europe the name of Benjamin Franklin was glorified. For he was truly a citizen of the world.